NECESSARY EVIL

By Shane Lacy Hensley

Art Direction, Graphic Design, & Layout:
Aaron Acevedo, Cheyenne Wright, Shane Hensley, & Thomas Shook

Proofing & Additional Help: Matthew Cutter, Norm "No Relation" Hensley, Preston DuBose, & Adam Loyd

Interior Illustrations: Aaron Acevedo, Ben Acevedo, Emma Beltran, Bien Flores, Alida Saxon, & Cheyenne Wright

Cover: Martin de Diego Sádaba

For Mark Valentine & Todd Breitenstein, who fought the ultimate evil.

WWW.PEGINC.COM

SAVAGE WORLDS

PINNACLE ENTERTAINMENT GROUP

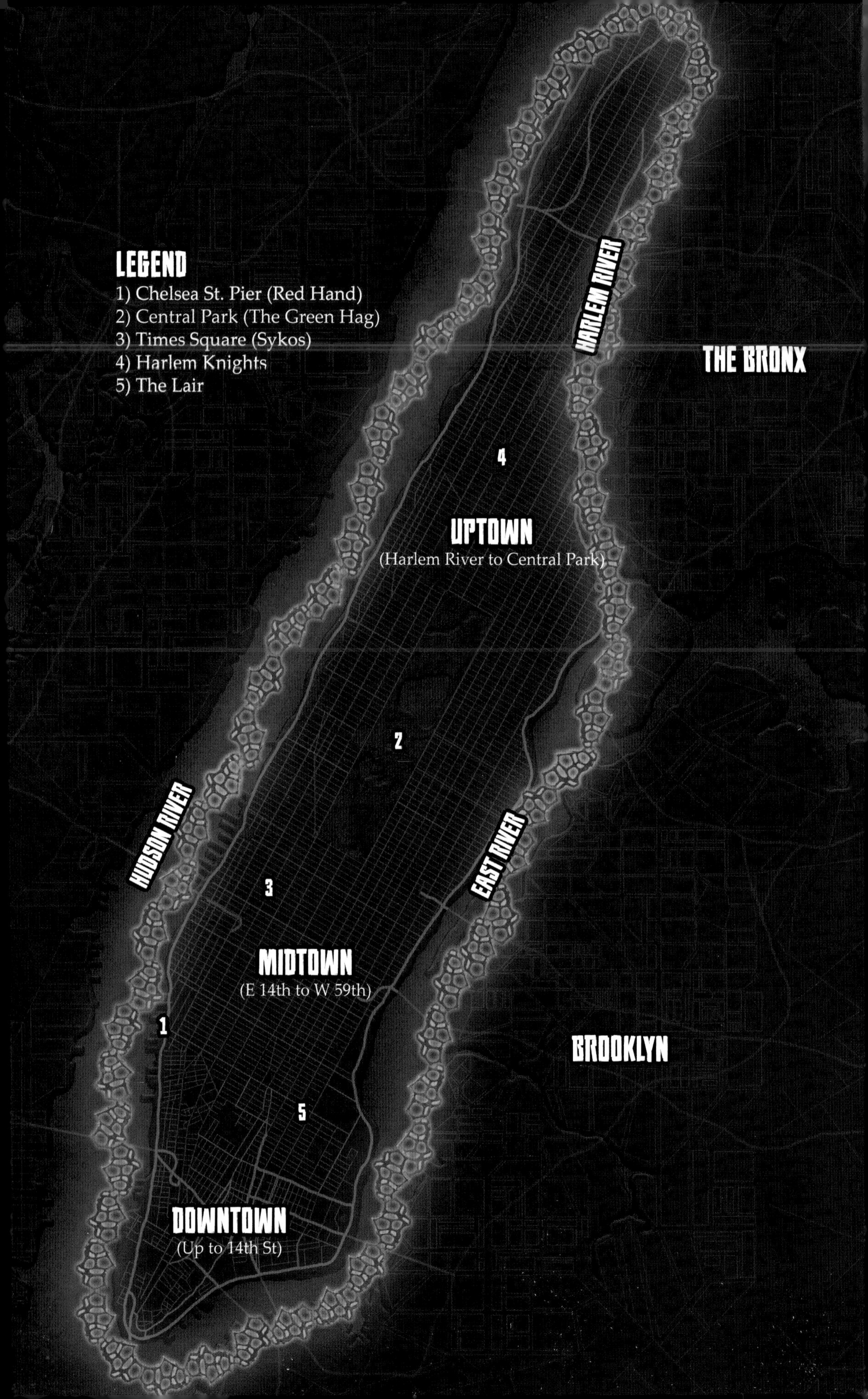
LEGEND
1) Chelsea St. Pier (Red Hand)
2) Central Park (The Green Hag)
3) Times Square (Sykos)
4) Harlem Knights
5) The Lair
HARLEM RIVER
THE BRONX
4
UPTOWN
(Harlem River to Central Park)
2
HUDSON RIVER
EAST RIVER
3
MIDTOWN
(E 14th to W 59th)
1
BROOKLYN
5
DOWNTOWN
(Up to 14th St)

TABLE OF CONTENTS

PLAYER'S SECTION

GAME MASTER'S SECTION

BREAKOUT

1/1/2001. That was the day the aliens attacked earth.

They dropped like steel rain from the dark void of space. Mysterious. Armed. Armored. Ferocious. Backed by a thousand armadas of fighters and bombers all across the whole wide world.

Most of the major cities fell in days, left in smoking ruins and streets soaked red with blood. Heroes rose. Ordinary men and women. Police forces. Soldiers. Sailors. Air forces. Marines. Super heroes.

But the aliens—horrifying creatures with shark-like faces and crocodile skin—were far more powerful. And they were legion.

Then came the v'sori. Allies to humanity, saviors of earth. They aided the heroes of the world in their struggle against the predatory invaders they called the *k'tharen*. Great battles were fought. Sacrifices were made. Secrets were shared. The v'sori–Earth alliance drove the merciless k'tharen horde back to the depths of space.

The survivors celebrated. The v'sori were given great ceremonies around the world. Dignitaries and super heroes gathered to shower them with gifts, praise, and gratitude.

The fools.

In a coordinated series of attacks across the globe, the v'sori proved not the foes of the voracious k'tharens—but their masters. The shark-men returned at the side of their insidious overlords.

Earth's heroes were caught off guard. Most were captured or slain in a single night of carnage and bloodshed. The rest, their identities and weaknesses cataloged during the false alliance, were hunted down in the weeks that followed.

Earth's armies, long grown overdependent on their super heroes, failed. Humanity was subjugated. The invaders wanted our resources and humans were tasked with providing them. In exchange, most of the world was allowed to rebuild and repopulate. Life slowly returned to some semblance of order, but always under the watchful eyes of the conquerors from the stars.

The aliens' plan to destroy the world's heroes and enslave its population was near total, but they hadn't counted on Earth's *villains.*

These selfish, vain, cruel, or megalomaniacal men and women had always rebelled against human authority, but alien rule proved intolerable. Soon they were united by a master criminal called Dr. Destruction. He formed these scattered malcontents into organized cells to fight the k'tharen warriors, thwart the v'sori, and eventually teleport to the invaders' home planet to fight their supreme leader—the monstrous Overmind.

That tale is told in the original *Necessary Evil* and focuses almost exclusively on Star City. But the v'sori battled across the entire planet, and there are many stories left to be told...

ESCAPE FROM NEW YORK

Star City had special protection from a god-like entity known as the Outsider. It was this cosmic entity who created the strange starburst-shaped island. His incredible psychic links shielded the land, causing painful backlash to the distant v'sori leader, the Overmind, for every bomb dropped or life lost within its boundaries.

No other cities on Earth were granted such protection. New York City, Paris, Hong Kong, and London were all but leveled in the initial invasion. Most other population centers suffered similar fates in the days to come. Every hero considered a significant threat by the aliens was carefully eliminated, either by the savage k'tharen in the early days or at the v'sori's treacherous "victory ceremonies" and mop-up campaign after.

By the end of 2002, the world was theirs.

EVIL RISES

The v'sori are known for the strange experiments they like to conduct on their conquered subjects. One of their favorite is to isolate a geographical area of interest with an unbreakable energy cordon and watch how the "insects" inside respond.

On May 15th of 2002, Sh'tarka, the v'sori Overlord of the New England, USA region, placed most of Manhattan under a cordon. The crackling blue energy field kills most anyone who comes in contact with it, regardless of their superpowers. Even teleporters have been stopped dead in their tracks at the edge of the barrier.

The cordon runs 100 yards off the shore of Manhattan on the Hudson River to the west and south, the East River to the east, and the Harlem River to the north. It rises 2,000 feet into the air, forming a roof above the tallest skyscrapers that prevents flying heroes, villains, or vehicles from entering or exiting, and as far anyone can tell, runs far beneath the muddy river beds as well.

Sh'tarka's shock troops patrol the outskirts, but so far the cordon has proven 100% effective. No one is known to have escaped, though several troublemakers have been thrown in. The v'sori drop ration bars throughout the city weekly, perhaps to avoid further dissent elsewhere, but more likely to watch the desperate survivors fight over them.

YOUR GOAL

Now the once-mighty Big Apple has become a collection of scavengers and the gangs who prey on them. The old mafia, the Red Hand, controls most of the remaining supplies. So-called "heroes" protect Harlem. A band of homicidal maniacs rules Times Square. A living entity made of rats grows ever-stronger in the sewers and subways. A thing called the Green Hag has taken over Central Park.

Your job as a villain is to escape from New York. It's just another prison to you, and no one—alien or man—keeps you penned up for long.

TIMING IS EVERYTHING

The v'sori betrayal occurred on April Fool's Day (April 1), 2002, a date chosen to cause the utmost confusion among at least some of their foes.

The original *Necessary Evil* starts in 2004—about two years after the v'sori took over. *Necessary Evil: Breakout*, officially begins on July 1st, 2002—two years before the events of the original story.

This should give most groups two years to finish the Plot Point Campaign included in this book. Of course the Game Master can also adjust those dates to fit her game as desired.

MAPS TO THE STARS

If you read the short story *Maps to the Stars* from our Wendigo Tales line, you know that a bloody reality show called "ARENA!" was staged in downtown New York City. That story is set up by some of the events in *Breakout!* and takes place afterward or near the end, depending on how the Plot Point Campaign goes. The Game Master has more information on this in **Arena!** on page 55.

MAKING VILLAINS

The k'tharen wiped out most of the truly powerful heroes and villains of New York. A few more escaped to join the resistance in Star City before Manhattan was sealed. That leaves an assortment of street-level villains, a few lone heroes and vigilantes, and a lot of civilians fighting for their very survival.

Player characters in *Necessary Evil: Breakout* are Street Level villains. They have 30 points to dedicate to powers. Use the *Savage Worlds Super Powers Companion* to make your nefarious evildoer. This book does *not* use the original *Necessary Evil* power section—those are now officially superseded by the *Super Powers Companion.*

Note that powers such as *altered form, flight,* or *teleport* are allowed, but they won't help the villain get through the cordon as it negates *all* powers that come in contact with it. Lethally. The Game Master has complete information on how that works in **The Secret of the Cordon** on page 34.

Here are a few other things you need to consider when making your super-powered criminal, mastermind, thug, or megalomaniac:

Restricted Edges: Characters may not take the Rich, Filthy Rich, or Noble Edges. All but a few important nonplayer characters are desperate scavengers in *Necessary Evil: Breakout.*

Seasoned Cretins: The villains of New York City have survived what slew most others. Make Novice-level villains with Street Level powers as described above. Once you are finished, give your villain four Advances to bring her to Seasoned Rank.

Motivated to Escape: All player characters must be eager to escape for some reason (or loyal to others who seek their freedom). Most simply want to leave the hellish conditions of ruined New York City, where power, entertainment, medical care, clean water, and simple luxuries like cable TV and fast food are a thing of the past. Some may have loved ones outside the dome they need to find. Some may simply resent their lack of freedom on pure principle—most villains are anti-authoritarian at heart, after all. A few may seek to escape just because they've been told they *can't.*

As you make your reprobate, figure out *why* she wants to escape. What drives her through the difficult days and terrible challenges that are to come? What makes her wolf down one ration bar for just enough energy to beat her foes senseless?

HEROES

Characters might also be heroes who somehow survived the v'sori invasion and subsequent surprise attack. They might also be more noble souls who gained their powers *after* the cordon was erected and now find themselves stuck inside the New York City Prison.

Use the same rules as the villains, above, to make your character. And good luck. Your companions are not likely very nice.

THE LAIR

The villains have secured a "lair" in the top floor of a seven-story building in Manhattan's Bowery district. The building stands at the corner of 2nd Avenue and 3rd Street, and used to have an Indian grocery on the ground floor. That was long since looted, but the smell of cloves and incense is there forever.

The owner managed to put solid iron bars on the windows before he fled for parts unknown, so it's reasonably secure.

The elevators don't work, of course, but the stairs are clear up to the 7th floor. The villains have already installed an iron gate with chain and padlock there. Each occupant has a key, and the Toughness of the bars, chain, and padlock is 16. The brick walls they're bolted to are only Toughness 14, however.

The group starts with whatever gear they've purchased plus two days' worth of ration bars and reasonably clean water.

Cockroaches and rats are frequent visitors, but otherwise the building is relatively sound.

THERE GOES THE NEIGHBORHOOD

At the start of the game, the villains have made a few other contacts in the neighborhood. Here's who they are and what they know. More information can be found in the Game Master's Rogues Gallery as well.

THE CONSORT

This former super villain was known as "The Consort of Crime." She was a serious hacker who could find out anything on anyone. "If it's out there, I'll find it," she used to say.

No one knows where the Consort has holed up, but most in the Red Hand or the Bowery know she can be reached via a mailbox on the ground floor of the building at 2nd and 2nd. A person puts their request for information in the box and walks away. The box is connected to some sort of pneumatic system and whisks the request away to the Consort's lair.

If she can find what the person is looking for, her underlings deliver a price in goods within 12 hours. These are deposited in larger mail boxes scattered around the city (it's different each time). Once payment is received, an underling delivers the sealed information within another 12 hours.

The Consort never asks for gasoline and seems to have access to the Internet, leading many to believe she has her own internal power source and a satellite, cable, or other line to the outside world.

GERVAISE

No one really likes this slimy, double-dealing polecat, but there's no denying he has a knack for hearing the latest rumors and news. Just remember that Gervaise likely knows *your* secrets too.

SHIVER

Shiver was once the Golden Dragon, a feared martial artist who fought on both sides of the law. He was horribly beaten and burned in the war with the v'sori and now shakes uncontrollably—hence the new nickname. He doesn't seem to take offense—and you'd know it if he did!

Shiver wanders the streets of the Bowery living off donations given to him by other scavs and gangers. Most honor the old master for his prior strength and the training he still manages to give on occasion.

If a hero or a villain wants to learn a few moves and shows the old master some kindness, they just might learn something.

TALIA

This gorgeous woman was a Wall Street exec before the war. Now she lives on the Bowery Street with her "Bowery Boys," a gang of about a dozen men and women who serve and protect her. They keep the neighborhood relatively peaceful, fighting off Sykos and the worst of the other gangs who stray into the area.

If Talia and the Bowery Boys can't defend the neighborhood, they've worked out a system of strongpoints, panic rooms, and hidden paths to get most of the residents out of harm's way.

Most of the neighbors drop a small portion of their scavenged goods on her doorstep for her help.

Talia's screenshot of the safe house before the internet went down.

GEAR

Villains may purchase equipment at the usual costs presented in *Savage Worlds* or the *Super Powers Companion* **during character creation.** All of the technology from the original *Necessary Evil* is listed below as well. Where there's a difference, use the updated versions here.

After character creation, the economy is based on trade and barter, with essentials (food, water, bullets) fetching far more than the usual cost. There are no cows in the cordon, for example, so there are no cheeseburgers—unless someone finds frozen beef somewhere. See the **These Prices Are Insane!** sidebar on page 10 to adjust prices once the game begins.

FOOD & WATER

Characters can't start the game with perishable foodstuffs—those were eaten months ago.

V'sori flying drones drop ration bars throughout the city once a week. The bars are near-flavorless, brown blocks of proteins, vitamins, and other nutrients. A single bar weighs three ounces and provides everything a normal person needs for a day's nutrition and calories.

Water is easy to find in ponds, cisterns, rain barrels, old toilet tanks and the like, but must be boiled or otherwise purified before it can be consumed. Don't be picky.

The Game Master should assume the villains find enough ration bars or occasional treats to survive, and as long as they have some downtime each day, can boil enough water to drink when needed. Track these things only if they become important.

OTHER PERSONAL GEAR

Holograph Projectors: Designed as plug-ins for modern computers and PDAs, these wondrous devices project a three-dimensional video image above the screen. (1 oz, $500)

Med-Stims: This remarkable nanotech device represents the pinnacle of human medical technology both before and after the v'sori invasion. Packaged in small, plastic tubular injectors, med-stims are pressed almost painlessly into the skin of the arm or leg and provide an immediate anesthetic treatment to nearly any injury. Tiny nanotech devices then go to work, traveling to the site of the most grievous injury and repairing the damage. Med-stims allow the recipient to ignore one point of wound penalties and increase the speed of natural healing to one attempt every hour, for up to three hours. Stacking doses has no additional effect, but is a waste of good nanites. Curiously, these same nanites *cause* 6d6 damage if injected into undead flesh, as Four Star and Lucky once discovered when battling the Vampire Kind. (6 oz, $1000)

THESE PRICES ARE INSANE!

New York City operates on a barter economy, with the value of merchandise essentially set by the Red Hand, which controls most of the goods in the city.

The prices listed in this chapter are the *normal* values one might find outside the cordon. Use the listed prices during character creation, when running your own *Necessary Evil* campaign outside the cordon, or if using the items in your own supers game.

After character creation in *Necessary Evil: Breakout*, adjust *all* prices as described below. Characters in the game actually exchange goods rather than money, but the Game Master and players should track their goods in dollar values for easier conversion.

- One ration bar is worth $10. Ration bars are dropped throughout the city by the v'sori and fought over by whoever gets to them first.
- A gallon of (relatively) clean water is traded for $10.
- Relatively nonperishable consumables such as canned or dried food, toothpaste, and toilet paper are worth 10 times their normal value.
- Gasoline sells for $50 per gallon.
- Consumables with short expiration dates such as fresh fruit, vegetables, or high-quality meat are worth 20× their usual value.
- Firearms and powered weapons sell for 50% of their normal value. Ammunition and battery packs sell for 10× cost, however.
- Hand weapons are worth their listed value.
- Tools are worth d6× cost because the owner knows the buyer must really need it or he wouldn't be asking.
- Cars are worth almost nothing, but motorcyles go for 10× list price (see **Mobility**, page 17).
- Art, gems, jewelry, and other non-essential luxuries are bought *only* by the Red Hand at a 10:1 ratio. A $10,000 painting, for example, is worth $1,000.
- Paper money is worth 1/100th its face value and again, only the Red Hand buys it. A $100 bill is thus worth $1.

ARMOR

All armor types from *Savage Worlds* are available in *Necessary Evil*. Armor types from the *Savage Worlds Super Powers Companion* are repeated below with some additional notes—and a few new selections as well.

Characters benefit only from the highest armor value worn unless otherwise noted.

Body Armor: Popularized by the highly successful DuraWeave brand, body armor is the staple of many spandex-wearing heroes and villains alike. This lightweight material can be worn under normal clothing with little inconvenience. It adds +4 Armor and negates up to 4 points of AP from ballistic attacks (but not energy or melee). (4 lb, $200)

Combat Armor: Worn by k'tharen troopers, v'sori elite, and anti-supers units, these suits include a full suit of armor with helmet and load-bearing harness for a backpack or other gear, boots, and gloves. The combat vest (5 lb, $300) and tactical helmet (2 lb, $100) may also be worn separately. Combat armor adds +6 Armor and negates up to 4 points of AP from ballistic attacks (but not energy or melee). (12 lb, $800)

Force Field, Personal: V'sori rulers have access to personal force fields, and a rare few of these have wound up in the hands of Earth's villains. Some of the latter were incorporated into "Z-Belts," named after tinkerer Arthur Ziggler, the developer.

Force field generators are typically worn as belts or backpacks and provide +4 Armor against all types of attack (except arcane). They're powered by enough energy for 24 hours of continuous use, then must be recharged for one hour. Force fields stack with all other types of armor except other personal force fields, and are not affected by AP. Note that recharging is very tough in the New York City Prison due to lack of electricity. (4 lb, $50,000)

Generator: A traditional generator costs $1,000 and provides 10,000 watts of power. It holds eight gallons of gasoline.

Riot Shield: Riot shields like those typically given to the police or paramilitary troops (including some v'sori) act as large shields (see *Savage Worlds*). Modern composite materials add +4 Armor versus ranged attacks instead of the +2 provided by those of earlier eras. (5 lb, $150)

CLOSE COMBAT WEAPONS

All the close combat weapons listed in *Savage Worlds* are available in *Necessary Evil*, and may be greatly enhanced by any one (and *only* one) of the upgrades below.

Gloves: The Energy Weapon, Power Weapon, and Stun Charge upgrades may be applied to gloves and gauntlets, providing enhancement to unarmed attacks. The base price for a glove or gauntlet is $5, and it weighs 1 lb. Gauntlets are included for free in full-body armor such as combat armor.

Power Packs: Some of the weapon enhancements listed below require "power packs." They continually recharge using a combination of kinetic motion, ambient radiation, and even body heat, but can burn out. On a 1 on the Fighting die, the power pack burns out and the weapon has no power until it is replaced, requiring an action. Each power pack costs $50 and weighs one pound. The weight of each enhancement below includes one attached power pack.

MELEE WEAPONS

Modification	Weight	Cost
Chain/Vibro Blade: Any bladed weapon, such as a sword or axe, can be fitted with a rotating chain of diamond-edged blades, or made to vibrate at extremely high frequencies. Chain or vibro blades are extremely loud, but add +1d6 damage and AP +2 to the weapon's basic statistics. Unpowered, the blade is a normal weapon of its type.	+2	$500
Energy Weapon: A weapon with a blade of pure energy or high frequency vibration. It increases the weapon's damage by one die type and grants +4 AP in addition to any other special abilities of the base weapon. Energy weapons have no minimum Strength limitation and count as a Heavy Weapon. They are unusable when unpowered.	+1	$500
Molecular Blade: Edged weapons such as daggers or swords can be given a monofilament, "molecular," or extremely thin edge, making them far sharper than usual. This gives the weapon +2 damage and adds half its damage die type in AP (+2 AP for a d4, +4 AP for a d8, and so on). Molecular blades require no power.	—	$500
Power Weapon: The weapon contains a variable burst of energy that's released on impact. It adds +1d6 to the character's damage. With a raise on the attack roll, the character's damage is a d10 instead of a d6. Power weapons function as their base type when drained of energy.	+1	$500
Stun Charge: Blunt weapons can be rigged to deliver a stunning charge of energy. After a target is hit by the weapon (including a Touch Attack), resolve damage. Then the victim must make a Vigor roll or fall prone and Incapacitated. At the start of each subsequent action, he makes a Vigor roll to revive. Success means he revives but is Shaken for the round and can recover on the next as usual. A raise means he revives instantly and is not Shaken. An unpowered stun weapon does normal damage.	+1	$500

PULSE WEAPONS

The v'sori and powerful human organizations use "pulse blasters," weapons that fire powerful bursts of energy at their target. A user can cause double damage with these devices by "focusing the charge" (a free action). This doubles the number of damage dice rolled, all of which may Ace. If a 1 is rolled on the Shooting die while overcharged, the weapon hits any **Innocent Bystanders** as usual (see *Savage Worlds*) then malfunctions and must be repaired (one hour, Repair −2) or replaced. Pulse weapons may cause lethal or nonlethal damage (attacker's choice).

Weapon	Range	Damage	AP	RoF	Shots	Weight	Cost
Pistol	10/20/40	2d6	2	1	24	2	$500
Notes: Power packs cost $20 and weigh .25 pounds each.							
SMG	10/20/40	2d6	2	3	24	2	$1,000
Notes: Power packs cost $20 and weigh .25 pounds each.							
Rifle, Sniper	40/80/160	4d6	4	1	12	6	$1,500
Notes: Min Str d6, Heavy Weapon, Snapfire. Power packs cost $30 and weigh .5 pounds each.							
Rifle, Assault	20/40/80	3d6	4	3	24	6	$1,500
Notes: Min Str d6, Heavy Weapon. Power packs cost $30 and weigh .5 pounds each.							
Pulse Gatling	20/40/80	3d6	4	3	48	12	$100K
Notes: Full Auto only. Min Str d8, Heavy Weapon, Snapfire. Power packs cost $50 and weigh 1 pound each.							

GRENADES

Earth-made grenades in *Necessary Evil* are lighter and easier to carry and throw than those listed in *Savage Worlds* (though those are available too).

The v'sori use grenades containing a micro fusion reactor capable of cracking tanks and super-powered beings alike.

Weapon	Range	Damage	AP	RoF	Shots	Weight	Cost
Fragmentation	5/10/20	3d6	–	1	1	1	$100
Notes: Heavy Weapon, MBT							
Fusion	5/10/20	3d10	2	1	1	1	$500
Notes: Heavy Weapon, MBT							
Stun Grenade	5/10/20	3d6	—	1	1	1	$100
Notes: Everyone in the area of effect must make a Vigor roll or fall prone and Incapacitated. At the start of each subsequent action, he makes a Vigor roll to revive. Success means he revives but is Shaken for the round and can recover on the next as usual. A raise means he revives instantly and is not Shaken. An unpowered stun weapon does normal damage.							

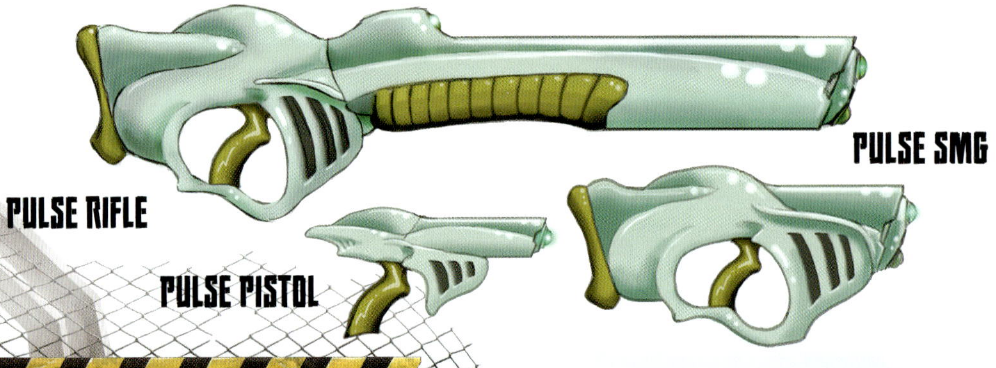

GYROJET WEAPONS

Gyrojet rounds have their own propellant, like miniature rockets, often used underwater but equally effective aboveground. Gyrojet weapons offer several types of warheads:

Armor Piercing: Damage 2d6, AP 10, Heavy Weapon.

Boomer: Damage 5d6, LBT, Heavy Weapon. Cost is doubled. Boomers have a minimum arming distance of 20" (40 yards) and can only be used in rifles.

Heat Seeker: Damage 3d6. Use the rules for missiles (see *Savage Worlds*), except the attacker uses Shooting and the defender uses Agility.

Rocket: Damage 3d6, Heavy Weapon. The basic line-of-sight projectile tipped with a microexplosive warhead.

Weapon	Range	Damage	AP	RoF	Shots	Weight	Cost
Gyrojet Pistol	12/24/48	By Type	—	1	10	3	$400
Notes: Heavy Weapon. Ammo costs $40 and weighs .5 pounds per 10 shots.							
Gyrojet Rifle	24/48/96	By Type	—	1	30	10	$600
Notes: Min Str d6, Heavy Weapon. Ammo costs $60 and weighs 1 pound per 10 shots.							

PLASMA WEAPONS

Plasma is superheated gas that can flash boil the flesh from a man or beast in the blink of an eye. Unlike a flamethrower, the fuel tank is stored in the weapon itself—usually in the form of energy rather than liquid propellant. When the trigger is depressed, the gas is heated and ejected as a small comet-like ball.

Weapon	Range	Damage	AP	RoF	Shots	Weight	Cost
Plasma Pistol	12/24/48	2d10+2	—	1	8	7	$600
Notes: Heavy Weapon, affects least-armored area, target may catch fire. Plasma packs cost $20 each and weigh .5 pounds.							
Plasma Rifle	24/48/96	3d10	—	1	12	12	$1,200
Notes: Heavy Weapon, affects least-armored area, target may catch fire. Plasma packs cost $40 each and weigh 1 pound.							

SLUGTHROWERS

Firearms are plentiful in the New York City Prison. Criminal gangs, police precincts, National Guard Armories, and even resistance fighters brought in most every type of weapon imaginable. For that reason, all the contemporary firearms listed in *Savage Worlds* are available in *Necessary Evil: Breakout*.

A new pistol, the M2-HeroKiller, is also available and was relatively common during the k'tharen invasion. Originally developed by Revile Industries in the 1980s for the burgeoning terrorist and secret society markets, the Mauser Magnum HeroKiller pistol, or M2-HK for short, fires overcharged tungsten-core bullets to penetrate the thick skins of the world's super-beings. Just before the v'sori claimed victory, a few M3-HeroSlayer rifles made it into the city as well.

Weapon	Range	Damage	AP	RoF	Shots	Weight	Cost
M2-HeroKiller	10/20/40	3d6	3	1	10	5	$300
Notes: Heavy Weapon. Ammo costs $50 and weighs 1 pound per 10-shot magazine.							
M3-HeroSlayer	20/40/80	3d10	4	1	10	10	$1,500
Notes: Heavy Weapon. Ammo costs $100 and weighs 2 pound per 10-shot magazine.							

SPECIAL WEAPONS

Weapon	Range	Damage	AP	RoF	Shots	Weight	Cost
Foam Thrower	10/20/40	Special	—	1	6	400	$2,000

Notes: Another wonder from the labs of Poseidon Dynamics, the POS-2 Foam Thrower Cannon was first employed during the 1999 Conference On Super-Genetics in Star City. This riot-control and containment weapon fills an area equal to a Small Burst Template with quick-hardening foam. Anyone caught in the area of effect must make an Agility roll versus the Shooting result or be caught. The foam is permanent until a solvent is applied or it suffers one wound (Toughness 10, blunt or cutting attacks only). For two shots (charges) per attack, the area affected is a Medium Burst Template, and for three shots it's a Large Burst Template.

Net Gun	5/10/20	Special	—	1	1	10	$500

Notes: Min Str d6. This shotgun-sized rifle with a bulbous barrel was developed by Seattle's Poseidon Dynamics in answer to a challenge by billionaire industrialist George Waits. A world-renowned precious metals speculator and philanthropist, Waits got tired of seeing anti-globalization protesters injured by riot policemen just trying to do their jobs. Poseidon engineered a rifle that fires a super-strong, but ultra-soft net synthesized from actual spider's silk. With a successful hit, the target is entangled. He suffers −2 to all actions and cannot move. He may try to break free with an Agility or Strength roll at −2. The net is Toughness 10, cutting attacks only.

Nullifier Gun	12/24/48	Special	—	1	4	5	$20,000

Notes: Amongst the weaponry of the v'sori, the nullifier gun is potentially the most terrifying for super-villains. This weapon fires a neutralizer ray that renders inert any natural or artificial energy signature. In other words, it takes away super powers! When hit, a target must make a Vigor roll or lose all super powers for 1d6 rounds.

Taser/Stun Gun	5/10/20	—	—	1	12	1	$300

Notes: After a target is hit, he must make a Vigor roll or fall prone and Incapacitated. At the start of each subsequent action, he makes a Vigor roll to revive. Success means he revives but is Shaken for the round and can recover on the next as usual. A raise means he revives instantly and is not Shaken.

Taser (Mega-Taser)	5/10/20	—	—	1	6	3	$10K

Notes: This weapon is a taser designed to deal with super powered individuals. It works exactly the same as the taser listed above, but the Vigor roll to resist is made at −2, or −4 if it hits with a raise.

FOAM THROWER

TASER / MEGA-TASER

SPECIAL AMMUNITION

Police forces, vigilantes, and villains have a few additional options when it comes to ammunition for their weapons.

Type	Weight	Cost	Notes
Rubber Bullets	—	—	Nonlethal damage.
Notes: Rubber or "mercy" bullets allow a firearm to cause nonlethal damage. They lose all AP bonuses, and have the same weight and cost as the weapon's normal rounds.			
Trick Projectiles	1/5	Varies	See below

Notes: Trick projectiles encompass any kind of thrown or launched projectile, with prominent examples including: arrows, billiard balls, boomerangs, darts, knives, and seemingly innocuous kitchen implements. The range varies according to the delivery system (i.e., a bow fires a trick arrow farther than a normal person can hurl a pool ball). The five most common trick projectiles are:

- **Adhesive:** Discharges a sticky, hardening goop that traps the target and holds him fast until he either breaks free or a solvent is applied. Use same rules as for the POS-2 Foam Thrower, but apply to single target. Cost: $50.
- **Bludgeon:** Ranged punch designed to incapacitate but generally not injure the target. Causes nonlethal damage. Cost: $1.
- **Concussion:** Delivers a charge of explosive or sonic force not unlike a close-range thunderclap, damaging and stunning the target with a deafening blast. The target must roll Vigor at −2 or be Shaken. Cost: $50.
- **Net:** Traps target in a super-strong nylon net that encloses on impact and grows tighter the more the target struggles. Use same rules as for the net gun, but apply to a single target. Cost: $100.
- **Rope:** Deploys a strong, super-thin nylon line up to 50 yards away allowing the firer to climb or swing his way across the city or out of imminent danger. Cost: $50.

VEHICLE WEAPONS

BLASTER CANNONS

V'sori vehicular blasters fire charged particle blasts with incredible penetration. Particles are filtered from ambient dust, water particles, or micro-meteors, granting unlimited ammunition when connected to a continuous power supply. If not, a power core can be attached providing 100 shots (the price is listed for each weapon below).

Weapon	Range	Damage	RoF	AP	Shots	Cost
Light	100/200/400	3d10	3	5	U	$100K
Notes: Heavy Weapon. Power cores cost $250.						
Medium	100/200/400	4d10	2	10	U	$500K
Notes: Heavy Weapon. Power cores cost $1,500.						
Heavy	100/200/400	5d10	1	20	U	$1M
Notes: Heavy Weapon. Power cores cost $3,000.						
Super Heavy	150/300/600	6d10	1	30	U	$1M
Notes: Heavy Weapon. Power cores cost $5,000.						

MISSILES/TORPEDOES

V'sori fusion missiles shred most conventional armor and forces. Sonic torpedoes detonate with a focused sonic blast. They are far more rare and usually only given to the biggest ships.

These weapons use the rules for missiles in *Savage Worlds* and require vessels with missile launchers or torpedo tubes to mount. Attackers use Shooting to get a lock if firing directly or Knowledge (Electronics) if fired indirectly from a bridge or weapons station. Defenders use Piloting (or Agility if they are a flying super) if evading directly or Knowledge (Electronics) if trying to jam or disrupt the missile lock. Determine lock by ship—if a ship gets a lock, it may fire all the missiles or torpedoes it's allowed. Ships evade each fired missile separately. A missile fired at Short Range hits that round if not evaded.

Weapon	Range	Damage	RoF	AP	Shots	Cost
Missile, Fusion	200/400/800	8d6	1	15	1	$200K/8
Notes: Heavy Weapon, MBT.						
Torpedo, Atlantean	100/200/400	8d10	1	30	1	$600k/8
Notes: Heavy Weapon, LBT. Watercraft only.						
Torpedo, Sonic	300/600/1200	8d12	1	40	1	$1M/8
Notes: Heavy Weapon, LBT. Space or watercraft only. Half Range in water.						

WAVE BLASTERS

Wave cannons are vehicular weapons that fire "bubble streams" of force through water. The bubbles have no armor penetration whatsoever, however, and the bubble field dissipates quickly at range, especially above water. They have unlimited ammunition when connected to a power source; on its own, a power core is good for 50 blasts.

Wave blasters halve their Range above water.

Weapon	Range	Damage	RoF	AP	Shots	Cost
Wave Blaster	30/60/120	3d8	3	—	U	$60K
Notes: Heavy Weapon. Power cores cost $250.						

VEHICLES

All the contemporary vehicles listed in *Savage Worlds* can be found throughout the city. Most military vehicles were destroyed or taken away after the v'sori victory. Gasoline is more problematic. A gallon costs $50 and is in short supply.

ARMORED TRUCK

Various gangs occasionally use armored bank trucks as armored personnel carriers.

Large Vehicle: Acc/TS 10/20, Toughness 21 (8), Crew 1+11, Cost $40K.

Notes: Heavy Armor +4, Crew Space, Reinforced Chassis.

CITY BUS

City buses are hard to maneuver in the packed streets, but a few of the gangs use them. Most weld steel plates around the sides. If so, add +4 armor all around.

Heavy Vehicle: Acc/TS 5/15, Toughness 20 (5), Crew 1+55, Cost $42K.

Notes: 12× Crew Space.

YASCHUK AERODYNE FLYING CAR

Yaschuk Aerodyne was the first pre-invasion vehicle developer to come up with a commercially available flying car. Using advanced hovercraft technology, the YA-1 was fast and versatile but expensive to build and quickly became a status symbol amongst the rich and famous.

Because of its versatility, the YA-1s were adopted by many super heroes and super villains, and after considerable modification became flying engines of destruction.

Medium Vehicle: Acc/TS 30/300, Climb 2, Toughness 12 (3), Crew 1+3, Cost $120K.

Notes: Anti-Grav

SETTING RULES

Necessary Evil: Breakout introduces two new Setting Rules, Mobility and Scavenging, that allow characters to move about the city and find junk, needed goods, or even incredible valuables in the ruins of New York. This is critical in a setting where the economy has broken down to a barter system.

All the Setting Rules presented in the *Super Powers Companion* are also in effect for *Necessary Evil*, including:

- **Comic Book Combat:** Includes **Combined Attacks** (characters can combine super powers to cause greater damage), **Finishing Move** (villains cannot be automatically killed when helpless—attackers get The Drop instead), **Knockback** (victims are sent flying by super-powered attacks), and **Synergy** (powers can be combined for additional effects).
- **Death & Defeat:** Characters draw on the Defeat Table when "killed" to see what actually happens to them.
- **Power Stunts:** Villains can temporarily use their abilities to mimic other powers.
- **Power Tricks:** An attacker can take a penalty to trigger different effects on her foe.
- **Super Strength:** Very strong villains and heroes can lift and carry enormous weights, and hurl heavy objects as weapons. Strength above d12 also doubles throwing Range for grenades and the like.

MOBILITY

The streets of New York are clogged with cars, toppled buildings, craters, and other reminders of the k'tharen and v'sori assaults. Getting anywhere in a car is almost impossible in any of the downtown areas without a rare Yaschuk "flying car." Only two are known to remain in NYC. Iron Head Tony of the Red Hand has one, and the Harlem Knights have another.

Motorcycles, however, work quite well and are in high demand, though Top Speed is generally limited to about 24" as the driver has to weave between obstacles and rubble.

The best ways to get around the city are flying, walking, and swinging. Flying and walking are at the character's normal Pace. Those with the *swinging* power can get just about anywhere in Manhattan at a Pace of 12".

If the Game Master needs to know how high up a character was when swinging or flying, such as if attacked, roll a d20 × 10 feet. Roll a d10 if the character says she's staying low, but double travel time since swingers can't get as much momentum and flyers have to stick to the streets and can't fly over the lower buildings and other obstacles.

Scavenging Table

Mishap or Critical Failure	The villain stumbles into trouble. The Game Master should consult the **Mishap Table** on page 25.
Failure	The miserable soul finds $2d10 worth of junk someone else didn't think was worth taking with them when they fled the city.
Success	The scavvie finds 1d10 × $50 worth of general goods, from valuable toothpaste to aspirin to diapers.
Raise	The villain may choose one of the following options: • **Loot:** The scavenger finds 2d10 × $100 worth of general salvage. • **Necessity:** The villain finds a specific (but non-unique) item he was looking for. The item must be relatively common before the invasion such as a blowtorch, a full reload of his weapon, a holoplayer, a particular category of medicine, the batteries he needs for a specific device, etc.
2nd Raise	**Rare Find:** The character finds something truly unique. The Game Master checks the results on the **Rare Finds Table** on page 26. Note that not every such treasure is just lying around waiting for someone to pick it up…you've been warned, miscreant!

Scavenging

Life within New York City depends on one's ability to make deals, gather allies, defeat enemies, and scrounge for scraps in the ruins.

There were over a million and a half people in all of Manhattan before the war but there are less than 50,000 now. The remaining inhabitants have picked the city over, but there's still lots of salvage to be found for those brave enough to prowl through the blasted buildings.

Valuables

Characters can scavenge for goods anytime they like. There are lots of items lying around the city that might prove useful to the survivors, or valuable to the Red Hand.

It's a lowly profession for those gifted few with super powers, but sometimes necessity requires scrounging through the ruins like a mangy rat.

The Game Master has information in her section for rewarding salvage based on completing certain adventures and defeating threats (see **Scavenging** on page 24), but villains can also spend their time scavenging just like the rest of the pathetic souls trapped in the cordon.

Values listed in the Scavenging Table or Savage Tales are *always* at the inflated NYCP prices unless it says otherwise.

To do so, each desperate scrounger spends four hours searching, makes a Survival roll, and consults the **Scavenging Table.** A Mishap is a failure with a 1 on the Survival die and triggers an event (Game Masters see **Mishaps** on page 25 to inflict pain and suffering on your sniveling scavs.)

The value of any salvage found is what it can be sold for. If a character finds $150 worth of junk, for example, he can use it just like cash and trade it for $150 worth of other junk. Remember the Red Hand only pays 10% of the value of works of art, cash, and the like—non-negotiable.

Selling Salvage

"Salvage" is a generic term that works just like cash. Characters may also find specific items they want to sell as well. In that case, figure the current real world price then check the sidebar These Prices are Insane! on page 10 for the multiplier (if any).

Selling to the Red Hand is automatic, but since they resell items, they only pay half price (or 75% with a raise on a Persuasion roll). Finding a buyer besides the Red Hand requires a Streetwise roll (and generates an Encounter for the area the character targets). Success on the Streetwise roll nets 75% of the value, and a raise nets 100%. This takes 1d6 hours per attempt.

GAZETTEER

New York City is nothing like Star City (setting of the original *Necessary Evil*), where life has been allowed to return to some semblance of normal. On that very special, star-shaped island, there are laws, police forces, and even a modicum of diplomatic interaction with the v'sori Warlords. New York City is a chaotic prison where the only rule is "might makes right."

The Big Apple was bombed extensively during the initial k'tharen invasion, but the real damage was done when the k'tharen champion Overbite battled the alpha-level hero Iron Maiden. The two mega-powerful supers destroyed dozens of square blocks; toppling skyscrapers, demolishing streets, and causing untold fires and explosions throughout the boroughs.

Hundreds of thousands evacuated then, and less than half returned by the time of the second invasion of the v'sori themselves.

K'tharen strike teams mopped up any remaining heroes in New York, then turned to the villains once the Omegan resistance in Star City began to take shape. But those proved more troublesome. When the shark-men and drones failed to secure New York, Warlord Sh'tarka placed part of the troublesome city under the ultimate v'sori sanction—the cordon. Whether this is security, retaliation, or experimentation doesn't really matter to the trapped inhabitants.

THE CORDON

The rest of New England has been allowed to rebuild, but the part of Manhattan within the cordon's energy field remains a ruined waste. The cordon starts at the Harlem River in the north and runs along both coastlines to the southern end of the island. Those who can fly say it reaches above Manhattan's tallest skyscrapers, and those who can tunnel or swim say it plunges at least 100 feet down into the island's bedrock.

The area it encompasses has come to be called the New York City Prison (NYCP). The v'sori provide some basic necessities to the prisoners in the form of ration bars to mollify the rest of Earth's troublemakers, but everything else is up to the forgotten survivors inside.

V'sori guards can come and go through the field as they please. Those of a scientific bent believe the field is somehow keyed to the aliens' DNA—or perhaps has a sort of ambient AI to determine when to open and close. No human, Atlantean, or non-v'sori has so far been able to breach it. Even teleporters or those who can take the shape of water or air have failed to pass through the cordon.

Experimentation with the cordon is incredibly dangerous. Those who touch the field suffer what looks like an electrical shock—but even those with electrical powers cannot survive it.

MEAN STREETS

The NYC Prison doesn't just run north to south and east to west. It also runs vertically, from the tops of the highest skyscrapers to the reeking depths of the sewers.

Gangs and super-powered individuals rule these levels and districts, from Uptown to Downtown and everywhere in between. Smart survivors learn which ones can be dealt with, which ones should be avoided, and which should be beaten to a pulp—before they strike first.

ABOVE

The Buzzards, cybernetically enhanced gangers with electric wings and powered razor claws, control NYCP's highest buildings (typically 10 stories or more). Civilians and gangs living in various buildings often use the lower roofs (10 stories or less) as lookout positions.

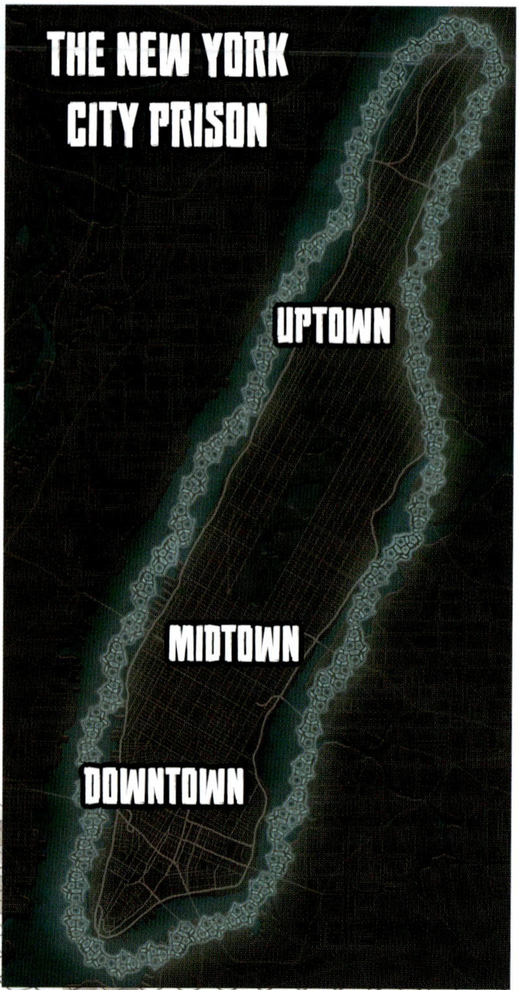

BELOW

A living carpet of rats called the Vermintide rules the underground tunnels. It is the most frightening foe in New York—which is saying something given Big Sis and the Green Hag.

No one knows much about the creature except that it appeared after the cordon was erected. The Vermintide dwells in the old subway tunnels, but erupts from manholes, sewer drains, and subway exits on occasion looking for meat. It is a ravenous, chittering wave of death to anyone unfortunate enough to be caught in its path.

Below the subway tunnels are the sewers. They flooded with seawater during the v'sori attack and have somehow become home to deranged and mutated k'tharen. No one, not even the Vermintide, enters what Iron Head Tony has called the "Red Depths."

UPTOWN

Upper Manhattan (Uptown) is bordered by the Harlem River in the north down to 110th Street and the Central Park border to the south, the river to the west, and FDR Drive to the east.

The Harlem Knights are the main power in this neighborhood. They were founded by former fireman Henry Jones, a no-nonsense member of the Harlem Firefighters. Jones leads a coalition of regular citizens and a few super heroes and reformed villains. The Knights have erected barricades around a series of former tenements in the northern part of Manhattan. There they've planted gardens, gather and boil rainwater, and are reasonably self-sufficient.

They aren't the most powerful of the gangs, but are fairly secure defensively and never leave the protection of their neighborhood without significant firepower and one of their three NYPD armored cars or black Yaschuk flying car. The Knights have a healthy supply of firearms, but rumor is ammo is getting short after numerous firefights with the Sykos.

MIDTOWN

Midtown runs from West 59th Street and the lower Central Park border to each coast and West 14th street. Times Square and the famous Broadway theaters are found here.

Most of Midtown is ruled by the Sykos, a band of chaotic malcontents who control what's left of Midtown and Times Square. They raid for supplies like most others but leave a wider trail of blood and misery in their path. They spend a lot of time warring with the "self-righteous" Harlem Knights but tend to avoid the organized firepower of the Red Hand.

Their leader is Big Sis, the most random and violent criminal in a sea of reprobates. Big Sis wears a variety of costumes ranging from "stripper nurse" to "pyromaniac welder," but the color combinations are always some mix of navy blue, blood red, and fiery orange. Her hair changes color *and length* on a near-daily basis, leading some to wonder if it's some strange aspect of her powers or simply a wide selection of wigs. Truth is, even before the v'sori came, no one knew what Big Sis looked like.

Sis has super strength and prefers big, nasty melee weapons in a fight. Spiked clubs and sledgehammers are favorite weapons, as are hurled manhole covers and mailboxes. She has even been known to pick up a mid-size car on occasion and smash her foes with it.

CENTRAL PARK

Central Park is technically part of Midtown but is its own kind of special. It's filled with fresh fruits and vegetables—which is strange because the flora that grow there are incapable of such produce. But the creature that dwells in the park, the Green Hag, uses her dark magic to tempt others into her domain. What happens to those who are caught trespassing, however, is anyone's guess—they are never seen again.

The Green Hag was the nemesis of Allan Fate, a hero who hunted supernatural threats before the war. Reporters said this dark druidess had taken the name of a mythical Irish witch named Irnan. Fate claimed she was actually the *ghost* of Irnan, who was slain by Finn MacCool in ancient Irish legends.

Whatever the truth, the Hag has transformed since becoming trapped inside the cordon. She is a darker, more sinister presence with all the powers and servants of the Celtic mythos at her command. Irnan appears as a floating wretch wrapped in flowing black tatters. At her feet are two phantom hounds, Bran and Sceolang—once the faithful pets of her ancient enemy. The Green Hag appears only at night, but her servant, a goblin-like villain called Aillen the Burner, watches over the park by day.

Whether their wrath is worth the succulent fruits and vegetables is a question locals ask themselves most every day.

DOWNTOWN

Lower Manhattan (Downtown) reaches from the southern edge of the island to West 14th Street. The Waterfront generally refers to the western edge of the island, where Iron Head Tony and the Red Hand have set up their black market fortress in the Chelsea Piers mall.

The Lower East Side includes the wharves to the east. They're in much worse shape and home mostly to beggars and scavs.

THE RED HAND

By far the largest and most powerful of the gangs is this group of former Mafiosos and mob hoodlums. They established their power right from the start with guns and plenty of muscle before anyone else could resist with similar force. The leader, Iron Head Tony, seized the Chelsea Piers waterfront mall and all the nearby warehouses, then tasked his extended "family" with filling it full of all the goods they could grab.

Now the Red Hand swells with food (ration bars, canned goods, and even some fresh fruits, vegetables, and meat), sells clean water, and even offers ammo, car parts, and other valuables brought to them by scavengers throughout the city.

Curiously, the Red Hand also takes in valuables such as jewelry, paintings, and even cash—at a 100:1 ratio. Some believe Iron Head Tony must have a connection to the outside for these treasures to have any value at all. Others say he's hoarding them in case the aliens ever decide to lift the cordon.

ROVING SUPERS

A few super-powered beings rove throughout the city and deserve special mention.

BLOCKBUSTER & GOLDEN GAL

Blockbuster and "GG" are true heroes who survived the v'sori betrayal because they weren't in our *dimension* at the time. They were part of a dimension-hopping super group called the Fabulous Five, and were off on some fantastic journey when the invasion occurred.

When they returned to our world New York was already in ruins. The fearless heroes jumped right into the fray, but one of their number, Golden Gal's husband, was killed in the first week. Two other members of the Five died over the next month.

The two heroes sulked for a while, but now they're back and looking for trouble.

Blockbuster is a massive bruiser with super strength and regeneration. Golden Gal is a powerful gadgeteer with an amazing suit of powered armor. Both heroes are considered well out of the league of street-level villains. You've been warned!

FULL AUTO

The New York City Police Department categorized the vigilante known as Full Auto as a full-on villain. He almost certainly thinks otherwise. This one-man killing machine preys exclusively on those he considers evil—particularly the Red Hand and the Sykos. He believes he is protecting the common man by hunting evildoers.

Villains had best beware should they see a man in gray or black urban camo carrying two full-auto submachine guns with an assault rifle on his back. He's put more "bad guys" in the grave over his long career than the local v'sori Warlord.

"I WON'T GO FULL-AUTO ON YOU. BULLETS ARE HARD TO COME BY THESE DAYS. JUST ONE WILL DO."

—FULL AUTO

NEVERMORE

Long ago, Nevermore was called the Raven, a young sidekick to a heroic vigilante called the Owl. His mentor was one of those heroes who would not kill under any circumstances, and paid for it. He died at the hands of a common thug after being driven mad by Dr. Phobos' mind-altering fear formula.

After that, Raven changed his costume and became the masked crusader called Nevermore. "Nevermore will we bow down before murderers and tyrants," he said famously before killing the previous leader of the Red Hand...Jackie "the Limo" Costanzo.

Since the cordon, Nevermore prowls the city, battling those he believes are the most cruel or terrible of New York's warring factions. He isn't particularly powerful, but he's clever and often prepares an area with traps, getaways, and weapons before engaging in a fight. Those who fight him would do well *not* to go where he seems to be herding them.

Nevermore is an ally of the Harlem Knights. He doesn't live with them but frequently helps out when they go to war with another gang, like the Red Hand or the Sykos.

GAME MASTER'S SECTION

GAME MASTER SETTING RULES

Now it's time to talk about the fun stuff, the rules you can use to torment your miserable miscreants! In this chapter you'll find the rest of the rules for Scavenging and the Mishaps and Rare Finds that can result.

SCAVENGING

Prowling around the ruins isn't what terrifying super villains with an agenda to escape the cordon should be doing, but sometimes they have no choice. And it can be rewarding on occasion. There are countless lost treasures lying in the detritus and debris of New York if you can get past the bones, rats, and ruins of the alien invasion.

The Game Master shouldn't encourage this kind of embarrassing behavior from his villains—they should instead be focused on breaking out of the cordon and stomping the v'sori into fine green paste. But should the team decide to crawl like dogs through the refuse of a dead city, here are the risks—and rewards—they run.

See page 18 for a reminder on the player's rules for **Scavenging**, then use the tables below for **Mishaps** and **Rare Finds**, or as inspiration for your own sinister ideas. Don't be afraid to get creative; the villains knew the risks when they started poking around the trash heaps.

MISHAP ENCOUNTERS

Several Mishaps involve enemies who would like little more than to tear the player characters limb from bloody limb. Whenever one of these is indicated, allow the villain who triggered the event to make an opposed Notice roll versus the threat's Stealth (a group roll if there's more than one foe).

- **Failure** means the threat sees the scavenger first and waits until he's isolated to attack. Allies may make Notice rolls each round to hear any resultant commotion, and can come to help their foolish friend the round after if they choose.
- **Success** means the villain and the threat see each other at the same time. The threat reacts as the Game Master thinks is appropriate. Allies may make Notice rolls and join the fight as above.
- **A raise** on the scavenger's Notice roll means she sees or hears the threat first and may act as she sees fit.

CHALLENGE ACCEPTED!

The results on the Mishap Table can be fairly light or *really* tough. They aren't designed to be a "fair fight." If the villains are outclassed or get unlucky, they must come up with a clever plan or run away. And if they overpower their foes easily? Let them revel in a violent victory. That's what being a power-mad psychopath is all about!

MISHAPS

Card	Mishap
2	**The Vermintide Awakens:** This is truly the worst thing that can happen. The scavenger disturbs a nest of rats directly connected to the Vermintide (see page 91). The swarm attacks immediately, and another swarm rises from cracks in the walls or holes in the ground at the beginning of each turn for the next 2d4 rounds.
3	**Collapse:** The floor, ceiling, supports, walls, or other structure collapses on the careless intruder. Roll Xd6 damage, where X is a d4+1. The careless clod gets one Strength roll at a penalty equal to −2 for every point on the d4. If this single roll is failed, he's trapped in the rubble and cannot free himself—he'd best hope his allies owe him a favor, or might want one in return. These are *villains*, after all.
4	**Scavs:** The villain isn't the only one prowling through the trash heaps. 2d6+2 other scavengers are about and decide to fight for the meager scraps lying about. Use the Scavenger statistics on 90.
5	**Chem Hounds:** A pack of chemical hounds have strayed from the old Hargrave Chemical Factory. 3d6 of the things attack. See page 82.
6	**Sykos:** A band of Sykos are up to no good nearby. There are 2d6 of the freaks. See page 91.
7	**Innocents:** Not everyone in the city is a miserable, selfish cur. A group of d6+2 civilians have found a Rare Find. They defend it as best they can, but won't risk their lives over it. Of course, they might follow anyone who takes it from them and plan to steal it (and everything else they find) later. Or they might make a deal with a rival, more powerful gang for a "finder's fee."
8	**Vermintide Hive:** Two swarms of Vermintide erupt from the ruins as the villains prowl through the garbage. If the Vermintide is ever dealt a Joker, another d4 swarms appear. The swarm is protecting its hive and will not retreat. See page 91.
9	**Vile Bile:** The group finds a stash of canned or packaged foods. Unfortunately, they've gone bad. Casual inspection reveals them to be "sketchy," but probably edible. Anyone who eats them must make a Vigor roll at −2 or get food poisoning, causing Exhaustion for the next 24 hours.
10	**Radiation Station:** The villains stumble upon a source of radiation. It might be a depleted uranium core from a US Army weapon, the power source of an android super hero or villain killed in the attack, medical waste, or even broken v'sori tech. Each scavenger must roll for radiation sickness as detailed in *Savage Worlds*. This doesn't serve Dr. Phobos' needs, however (see page 48).
Jack	**K'tharen Mutates:** 2d6 of these monstrous horrors are prowling through the ruins looking for food. See page 86.
Queen	**K'tharen Mutates:** 2d6+4 of these monstrous beings stalk prey in the ruins. See page 86.
King	**Vigilant Vigilante:** One of the city's vigilantes find the villains. Roll a d6: 1–2 Full Auto, 3–4 Nevermore, 5–6 either a group of 2d6 Harlem Knights, or the Judge if the Savage Tale Gang War! (page 68) is active.
Ace	**Risk & Reward:** Draw again, ignoring further Aces, but draw a Rare Find as well.
Joker	**Big Trouble:** Draw twice, ignoring Aces, and apply both results, but also draw a Rare Find. If two threats are indicated, they might be fighting with each, making a deal, squabbling over the Rare Find, or even stalking the villains if that fits the current narrative.

RARE FINDS

A red card (Hearts or Diamonds) indicates a local Encounter along with the treasure.

Card	Mishap
2	**The Lazarus Station:** It was rumored the hero known as Allan Fate, equal parts inventor and sorcerer and enemy of the Green Hag, created a device that would bring the dead back to life. In a hidden room somewhere in the city, the villains find his invention—the Lazarus Station. If a dead human (or Atlantean) is placed inside the device, he or she will return to the land of the living. It is powered by mystic crystals, and only one remains, however!
3	**Fuel Depot:** The villains find a significant supply of gas, perhaps located in a private industrial park's refueling station, a tanker, or other source others have passed by. There's 2d10 × 50 gallons for the taking.
4	**Armory:** The group finds a stash of weapons. Roll three times on the Weapons Sub-Table on page 27.
5–8	**Valuables:** The scavenger finds objets d'art, jewelry, or other valuables worth 2d20 × $1000. This is what the Red Hand will pay—the "real world" value is much higher. Choose or roll a d6 to determine the type of prize: 1–2 **Art:** A rare, expensive, or famous painting. 3 **Cash:** A significant stash of cold, hard cash, perhaps in multiple currencies like dollars and Euros, or gold, platinum, or silver ingots. 4–5 **Gems and Jewelry:** A private stash or unlooted jewelry store perhaps hidden behind other rubble. 6 **Sculpture:** A heavy (d6 × 100 lb) statue or physical piece of art. It might be of an historical figure, an abstract, or more likely, that of a super hero.
9	**Relics:** Each time this result occurs, roll or choose a different device (all powers are from the **Relic Sub-Table** on page 27).
10	**Gizmo:** In a sealed safe (Lockpicking −8 to open, one try only; or a welding torch or similar power), are schematics for a high-tech gizmo created by one of the city's super heroes or villains. The Game Master should pick a three-point power from the *Super Powers Companion* with the Device modifier.
Jack	**Shriek Box:** A deceased inventor created these matchbox-sized subsonic devices to repel the Vermintide. They last for one minute of use and cause the Vermintide to make a Spirit roll at −4 to get or stay within two yards of the wearer. Each time this result comes up finds one shriek box.
Queen	**Tiny Aphrodite:** The villain finds the android known as Tiny Aphrodite. The half-sized android attacks, but might be turned into an ally if she can be captured or Incapacitated. See 91 for more information. If this result comes up a second time, treat as **Valuables**.
King	**Force Field Generator:** The villain finds the corpse of a long-dead v'sori officer. His armor is crushed and his weapons are gone, but a careful look notes his personal force field (see page 10) is still intact.
Ace	**Vehicle:** Roll a d6. The group finds a v'sori mbuna (1–2), armored car (3–4), or Yaschuk flying car (5–6, cherry red, of course). It is mostly functioning but has two critical hits. Roll twice, ignoring any results that would destroy the vehicle.
Joker	**Isotope 23:** The villain finds a glowing chunk of what looks like turquoise. Any kind of scientific Knowledge roll alerts the finder as to its purpose. If it touches bare skin, the character makes a Vigor roll—no Bennies may be spent, however! If successful, the character manifests up to five points of new powers! If the roll fails, however, the villain gains the powers but develops a grotesque mutation that lowers his Charisma by −2. The mutation is usually an extension of his powers or personality.

RELIC SUB-TABLE

d6	Relic
1	**The Rocket Ace's Rocket Pack:** Rocket Ace's crushed remains lie buried in rubble, a victim of a savage k'tharen attack. With a Repair roll at −2, his pack can be made to work again. This gives the wearer *flight* with the Device modifier.
2	**The Revenant's Shroud:** This horrible, tattered shroud projects a 2d6 *damage field* and is Permanent. For one minute after taking it off, the character suffers −1 Fatigue from the heavy and oppressive feel it radiates.
3	**Shiner's Wrist Bands:** These crushed wrist bands are still wrapped around the bones of the hero who once wore them. They project sizzling beams of light, per the *ranged attack* power (Range 24/48/96, Damage 3d6, AP 2, Focus, Heavy Weapon).
4	**Minion #17:** A matter-controlling villain named Scrap Iron created an army of minions to fight the v'sori during the war. For some strange reason, one of them survived. The creature sits in some isolated location waiting for a new master to give it purpose. Have the scavenger make a Persuasion roll at −2 (ignore the penalty if the villain is haughty and demanding—just like Scrap Iron, which the character might recall with a Common Knowledge roll). If the roll is failed, the minion attacks. If successful, he serves the villain without question until his destruction. Use the statistics for the Matter Construct in the *Savage Worlds Super Powers Companion*. Its Strength is d12.
5	**Atlantean Spear:** In a museum, personal collection, or other protected place is a spear from the lost city of Atlantis. It causes Str+d10 damage, AP 4, and adds Parry +2.
6	**The Book of Al-Maalik (Partial):** In the ruins of a tumbled bookcase, the villain finds the remains of a decaying book. It grants the *super-sorcery* power at level 2. Reading the book (2d6 days at least) allows the character to spend an Advance to gain the Spellcasting skill.

WEAPON SUB-TABLE

Whenever a weapon is found, roll a d6 to see how much ammo or battery power it has: 1–2 Empty, 3–4 Half full, 5–6 Full.

d20	Weapon	d20	Weapon
1	A single modified hand weapon of the player's choice. She can choose from any of the standard effects listed on the **Melee Weapons Table** on page 11.	11	Roll again. The find is actually ammo or battery packs for whatever weapon is rolled instead of an actual weapon.
2	d4 × M16 A4	12	Net Gun
3	d6 Frag Grenades	13	Nullifier Gun
4	d6 Fusion Grenades	14	Mega-Taser
5	d6 Stun Grenades	15	Pulse Pistol
6	Plasma Pistol	16	Pulse SMG
7	Plasma Rifle	17	Pulse Rifle
8	M2-HeroKiller	18	Gyrojet Pistol with d6 random warheads
9	M3-HeroSlayer	19	Gyrojet Rifle with d6 random warheads
10	POS-2 Foam Thrower	20	Player's choice of any result on this table.

STAR CONQUERORS

Thousands of years ago, a semi-aquatic species of aliens called the v'sori fled their dying world and settled on Earth. The scientist who perfected space travel and saved his species was called Ch'thadra.

Ch'thadra and the other senior leaders even built a great city—Atlantis—and ruled over the primitive humans who dotted the nearby shores in crude towns and villages.

V'sori are telepathic creatures, and those with more natural abilities had always ruled those with less. Ch'thadra, for all his genius, had the psychic strength of a "kranth," a derogatory term that translates to something like "child," or more accurately "tadpole."

Over time, Ch'thadra the Tadpole was supplanted by the more psionically powerful v'sori of Atlantis. He did not take this well. Had he not saved their entire species? Had he not constructed the technology that built great Atlantis? He had little room in his tremendous brain for psychic powers, Ch'thadra told his detractors, it was too full of *science!*

Though some nodded in agreement, the scientist never truly regained his status. So he turned to the one thing that had always worked for him—technology. If he was not *born* with great telepathic powers, he would create them!

The first results were tragic. Subjects lost their minds, became vegetative, or developed warped personalities. But Ch'thadra would never stop. He could not figure out how to grant psionic powers to test subjects, but he did eventually learn how to *siphon* it from others and channel it into a living receptacle.

Ch'thadra, still the city's First Architect, built conduits throughout the great city. Every citizen on the vast island would feed his machine. The tadpole waited, stole their energy, and did his best to conceal his wry smile when anyone wondered why the Atlanteans were slowly losing their abilities.

Finally his psychic power cells were full to bursting. Ch'thadra hooked himself to the batteries and threw the transferral switch.

The scientist's mind absorbed all it could but even his massive brain was like a sponge trying to absorb an ocean. The resulting backlash raced through the conduits of Atlantis and triggered a massive earthquake. Within hours, the Earth's first great city began to sink into the sea.

The surviving Atlanteans knew what Ch'thadra had done as their stolen psyches came flooding back. They attacked his lab, but the monstrous creature that emerged from the blasted hole in the ground was far too powerful. The scientist now had a massive swollen brain, blood-red eyes, and horrible claws surging with psychic energy!

Ch'thadra killed dozens, then retreated to the old v'sori spaceships with as many minds as he could enslave. Over three hundred

Atlanteans vanished into the stars that day, never to be seen on Earth again.

When the smoke cleared, some of the remaining Atlanteans attempted to rebuild their city under water. Others assimilated into the human cultures. In time, Ch'thadra became nothing but a dark legend used to scare children—it was but one event in millennium of hardships, after all. Before the attack on Earth, most Atlanteans considered the legend of Ch'thadra no more real than Romulus and Remus' founding of Rome.

THE OVERMIND'S REVENGE

Ch'thadra did not spend his self-exile idly. Now calling himself the "Overmind," Ch'thadra had the combined intellect of all the minds he'd once held. As the millenniums passed, he and his minions developed a new society, super-weapons, and an unimaginable space fleet. The v'sori conquered the neighboring galaxies and enslaved all the races they encountered. The Overmind devoured more knowledge and psychic energy, becoming the most powerful psionic in the entire universe.

One of the races the v'sori encountered were a meek people brimming with latent supernatural abilities—the proteans. Rather than fight, the proteans fled. Most were slain, but one ship managed to slip away to Earth. They sensed the attackers had come from this distant planet and hoped the key to defeating them might be found there.

The protean ship was damaged in its flight and crash-landed in Siberia in 1908. The crater it made has come to be called the Tunguska Blast. The surviving proteans used their abilities to disguise themselves as human beings and lived in a single remote village near the crash site for several years.

There they prayed to their distant god, the Outsider. He slowly communicated his desires to his chosen people by dreams and visions: to go forth and multiply. Since the visions began, the proteans were haunted by one strange image they didn't understand until 1955—the image of an eight-pointed star. The obedient proteans did as they were instructed, however, and for nearly a century interbred with humans. The children of these pairings inherited a portion of their alien parent's power, though it rarely manifested except under extremely stressful situations.

STAR CITY IS BORN

One sunny day in 1955, the people of Earth awoke to find a titanic being standing in the water two miles off the coast of New York City. The super hero known as Silver Sentinel rushed off to greet the giant, and when he was swatted away, retaliated with shimmering high-energy blasts. The Outsider fought back, and what happened next was lost to the circling aircraft cameras in the massive tidal waves their battle created.

When the spray finally settled, the Outsider was gone and Silver Sentinel lay unconscious on a new land mass that hadn't existed before. The island was shaped like an eight-pointed star.

INFLUX

The surviving proteans, ageless creatures that they were, recognized not only their god, but his sign—the creation of an island in the shape they had seen in their dreams for nearly half a century.

Most of the proteans moved to Star Island immediately and continued procreating as their deity desired. Though the purpose of the island is still unknown to them, they have faithfully created a large number of progeny to fill it, many of whom have developed incredible super powers when faced with extreme duress. Most of the super beings fought for the good of the world, but many were also selfish souls who used their gifts for personal gain.

The story of Star City and its resistance to the Overmind is told in the original *Necessary Evil,* available from www.peginc.com or your local game store.

RULE OF THE OVERMIND

The Overmind is the ultimate commander of the v'sori. He never ages, and in fact seems to grow more powerful as his massive intellect absorbs more and more psychic energy from the worlds he conquers. Retaking Earth is his ultimate prize, for though the Atlanteans have forgotten him, he has not forgotten them. Nor has he forgotten how they ridiculed him for his lack of psionics or attacked him when he tried to augment his powers through science (at least, that's Ch'thadra's version of events).

The Overmind had an irrational fear of taking Earth and put it off for centuries, waiting until his fleet was so vast and his powers so strong he could not be defeated. His scouts have been here for years—some even tried to help the Nazis take over the world in 1941—but the rising population of super heroes proved troublesome. The Overmind waited patiently until he believed his plan to eliminate the world's super beings and demolish Atlantis was faultless.

As detailed in the original *Necessary Evil*, his fears proved justified despite his long delay and many precautions. But that confrontation is yet to occur in *Necessary Evil: Breakout*. For now, the Overmind and his vast armies are firmly in control of the big blue planet called Earth.

F'ARAK, THE WAR MASTER

The Overmind appoints one of his most trusted commanders to govern each planet he conquers. The War Master of Earth is a cunning soul named F'arak. The wily veteran fought his way up through the ranks, earning his spot by his cleverness and willingness to pound an enemy with his minions relentlessly. Though v'sori do not often engage in direct combat themselves, F'arak has seen action on many occasions, and in fact lost an eye in a fight many years ago.

SHOCK LORDS

Beneath the War Master of Earth is a council of seven Shock Lords, one for each of the planet's inhabited continents (two for the heavily-populated Asia and none for Antarctica). These individuals attend the War Master at strategy meetings and help plan his highest-level operations.

All Shock Lords fancy themselves aspiring War Masters and attempt to impress the Overmind so that they might one day become War Masters themselves.

OVERLORD

The next step down in the v'sori hierarchy are the Overlords. They typically watch over nation-size regions and are primarily concerned with logistics and administrative matters.

Overlords are almost always despised as "useless middle-men" by both their superiors and the Warlords who report to them.

WARLORDS

Warlords bear the real responsibility of ruling the planet's conquered populace. They're responsible for "districts" carved out by their Overlord. The size of a district is based more on the amount of trouble or resources a place generates rather than pure area. One Warlord rules Star City, for example, another New England, and another the entire American Northwest.

"THIS PLANET AND EVERYTHING ON IT IS MINE!"

—THE OVERMIND

MINIONS

The subjects of the Overmind are numberless. Entire armies rule over distant planets and even systems in the vastness of space. Some of these troops are v'sori, some are the shark-like k'tharen, some are cyborg slaves, and some are even mercenaries made up of brutal alien races still unknown on Earth.

Below are the most common soldiers, servants, and other minions encountered in *Necessary Evil.*

TROOPS

Forces are allocated as needed, so there is no standard organizational chart for the v'sori. In a district with a high but docile populace, a Warlord might rely on nothing but a company or two of drones (see below) and a personal guard of Battle Masters. In a more troublesome area such as Star City or New York, troops are far more numerous.

V'SORI SOLDIERS

Common v'sori soldiers are considered fodder by their Warlord, but are at least above the far more common servitor species detailed below.

On occasion, v'sori soldiers have rebelled against their societal "betters" and caused their Warlord significant embarrassment. For this reason, most commanders prefer to rely on the more loyal Battle Masters, less intelligent k'tharen, or barely sentient drones.

There are few legions of actual v'sori soldiers on Earth. The paranoid Overmind wisely feared the common men and women of his species might take sympathy on their ancestors, particularly the Atlanteans.

BATTLE MASTERS

Battle Masters are heavily trained, unquestioning "special operations" troops. The v'sori use them to carry out particularly sensitive missions where some subtlety is called for (such as kidnapping or assassination) or when a particularly clever threat (such as certain super heroes or villains) must be taken down.

Battle Masters thus serve as spies, infiltrators, mind readers, assassins, and shock troops. They are equipped with whatever high-tech devices are believed necessary to carry out their assignments.

Older or injured Battle Masters are often placed in charge of prisons, bases, or other installations as needed.

SCIENTISTS

The v'sori are hungry for knowledge—particularly as it might help with conquering new planets. For this reason, the v'sori military is indistinguishable from its bureaucracy, and scientific pursuits are just another extension of their might.

V'sori are both a psionic and a technological culture, and the many worlds they have conquered have given them countless devices, powers, and insight. The head of a particular project is simply called the Chief Scientist in the human tongue. They do not formally use the term "Doctor," but some have adapted the Earth tradition and use it informally.

Most v'sori scientists are far more interested in knowledge than ethics. They have ranged so far, seen so much, and been conditioned from the earliest age to favor scientific inquiry over the "discomfort" of countless test subjects. The suffering of one planet—let alone one species or one individual—is nothing in the cosmic scheme of things.

V'SORI SERVITORS

Besides members of their own race, the v'sori have several servitors they've come to depend on. On Earth, these are the k'tharen, drones, and Quislings.

THE K'THAREN

When the v'sori began their expansion more than a millennium ago, the k'tharen were one of their first stops along the way. They were also one of the most difficult. The shark-like "fins," as the Earthers call them, fought so savagely against the technologically superior v'sori that the Overmind eventually decided to try a different tactic. He called for peace and offered them the blood and treasures of a thousand worlds in exchange for their service. Eventually, the fins agreed.

Fins do not rely on guile or craft to win their battles. Though an intelligent and cunning species, they become frenzied berserkers in battle. They attack foes in waves of slavering berserkers, usually after the v'sori air forces have bombed an opponent's frontal defenses into submission. Fins use their tremendous size and toughness to great advantage, pressing frontal assaults that would be suicidal for lesser beings.

DRONES & WAR SPHERES

These poor souls are the epitome of a "fate worse than death." When the v'sori need completely obedient slaves, they subject captured foes to horribly precise lobotomies that strip them of their independence. The mind inside cannot refuse its commands, betray the v'sori, or otherwise act against its masters, but it knows exactly what it's doing!

Most drones are a very uniform size of six feet tall and completely cloaked in armor made of advanced polymers. This makes them look like robots, which is what the v'sori claim, but rumors of the truth are rampant.

Hyper drones are augmented further, and used only in extreme cases away from conquered populations. They are cyborgs with wires and cybernetics plugged directly into their dying flesh. The process burns them out quickly, but they are powerful foes while their bodies last.

The v'sori also make drones called "war spheres," flying metal balls of death they also claim are robots. The truth, of course, is that the spheres are "crewed" by captured brains just like the more humanoid drones.

The vast majority of drones on Earth are human, though there are still a few legions of aliens left over from the original attack. These are drawn from a humanoid race conquered just before the current invasion.

Collectively, there are well over 100 million drones on the planet at this time, with 90% of those made from humans.

QUISLINGS

A disturbing number of humans have willingly volunteered to work for the v'sori. They function as "gangs" and are used primarily for the aliens' amusement. There are no Quislings in Necessary Evil: Breakout, but they are common in other areas of the world. Use statistics for Gangers (page 84) if you want to introduce these traitors into your campaign.

WARLORD SH'TARKA

The Warlord of the New York area is Sh'tarka. She and her guards maintain a base just outside NYCP at the former Riker's Island Prison. There she has a legion of 5,000 drones, 100 hyper drones, and 1,000 war spheres to oversee the New England region.

When a threat is more serious, Sh'tarka has five teams of five Battle Masters. She also has five "pods" of 100 k'tharen each. One in 10 of these is a k'tharen commander. Any time a situation requires more than a dozen k'tharen, a Battle Master is sent to lead them.

Sh'tarka also has a number of Quisling gangs throughout New England, human toadies who have sworn allegiance to their alien overlords.

The Riker's Island base has a hangar with a half-dozen manta fighters and two dozen mbuna transports. Sh'tarka can quickly requisition up to 10 times that from the surrounding regions if necessary.

Should something go truly wrong, v'sori reinforcements from numerous man-o'-war battleships in orbit above North America arrive in under 45 minutes.

PATROLS

A v'sori Battle Master patrols the perimeter of the NYCP via mbuna transport. On board are a half-dozen k'tharen. The transport has no regular route and isn't very methodical in its duties—the aliens' trust in the cordon is absolute.

THE MANHATTAN PROJECT

Sh'tarka has told the Overmind and her peers that the New York City Prison is just another experiment designed to understand the super villains and their behaviors.

This is true, as far as it goes, but Sh'tarka has a much more treacherous plan in mind as well—the island is the training ground for a new breed of k'tharen warriors loyal only to her, and resistant to her species' psionic powers!

Sh'tarka believes the Overmind is insane. The resources spent to capture this one backwater world—and the difficulty they're having in doing so—has convinced her it's time for a new Overmind. Of course there is no better candidate to Sh'tarka…than Sh'tarka!

But to overthrow a being as powerful as the Overmind requires a small but elite band of warriors who can penetrate the Overmind's flagship and stave off his phenomenal psychic powers.

SUPER SOLDIERS

Sh'tarka and her lead scientist, M'oro, have been injecting protean DNA into k'tharen embryos, which are then grown to adulthood in just a few days via v'sori super science. Sh'tarka just needed somewhere to hide the laboratories and breeding vats.

During the attack on New York City, her agents discovered a forgotten submarine pen deep beneath the city. It had been created by a mad Nazi scientist during World War II and shut down by the heroes Four Star and Lucky. Sh'tarka assigned M'oro and a team of her most loyal soldiers to repair the base and begin the breeding program. Then she created the New York cordon to better ensure her rivals wouldn't discover her plans.

So far, the k'tharen test subjects have emerged with super strength and ferocity, but also debilitating mental mutations. M'oro

unleashes a few at a time into the streets above to test their abilities.

M'oro is very loyal to Sh'tarka, not out of love or admiration, but because he knows that if he fails, the Warlord will destroy the sub pen and all trace of her attempted treachery—including him! Only if Sh'tarka is successful in overthrowing the Overmind will M'oro regain his freedom from the dark depths of his hidden lab. And possibly rule by her side as well!

THE THARN

During the *Breakout!* Plot Point Campaign, M'oro is successful in breeding this new type of fin super soldier, called the "tharn." These black-skinned k'tharen are not only resistant to psionic powers but have developed the ability to encase their teeth and claws in psychic energy to cause much greater damage than others of their kind.

See page 87 for more details.

THE SECRET OF THE CORDON

The cordon is a force field, but it's far more than that. It's a *living* force field infused with trillions of microscopic, semi-sentient, living creatures. The beings are psionic and can sense the thoughts, auras, and even electromagnetic energy of any sentient being.

Anyone on their approved list is let in or out of the cordon at will. Anyone *not* on the list is subject to the massive energy of the force field being channeled directly into their person. If that doesn't work, the creatures channel psionic energy into the trespasser.

Either way, the attack causes a flat 50 points of damage—more than enough to kill most threats.

The field can also absorb 50 points of damage. Damage in excess of that (in a single attack) causes a temporary shudder in the field in a 2d6- by 2d6-foot hole. Roll a d6 each round thereafter. On the first round, the hole closes on a roll of 1, then 2, and so on until it closes. (Each roll of 6 keeps the breach open.)

Despite rumors to the contrary, a few large bombs and blasts *have* created holes in the wall. Early on, a few heroes and villains (of the Four Color power level) actually escaped this way. Several attempts afterward have had near success, but the v'sori react quickly if they sense anyone tampering with the field. On the occasions it's been tried, v'sori strike teams waited just outside the opening to kill anyone who tried to come through (there are no second chances here). Other attempts have occurred high in the sky or below the river's surface, but have resulted in similar but less well-known catastrophes.

This is why the captives of NYCP have so far not found a way to escape—the nanobeings know when non-approved individuals attempt to cross the barrier and instantly respond with lethal force.

"NO ONE GETS OUT. NO ONE."

—SH'TARKA

THE NEW YORK CITY PRISON

The player's section of this book gives a good overview of what most inhabitants of the NYCP know about the various gangs and miscreants who rule the island. But there is far more you should know before bringing these black-hearted malcontents into your campaign.

On the following pages is more detailed information on the various areas of the New York City Prison, its inhabitants, and the trouble your malevolent malefactors are likely to get into.

✦ **Savage Tales:** Entries marked with a star indicate an associated Savage Tale (short adventure) on the listed page.

New York City Prison is divided into five major areas: Above, Below, Uptown, Midtown, and Downtown. There are numerous areas within as well, such as Central Park, the Bowery, the Lower East Side, and Broadway.

Each section also includes an Encounter Table. Generally, the Game Master should generate an encounter any time the villains visit the area for any significant time and don't have another encounter planned.

If the encounter is a threat of some kind, make Notice rolls for both groups (the player characters and the foes). The highest roll sees the other first—and is unseen by the other with a raise. (Subtract 2 or 4 from a side's roll if the opponent is particularly stealthy—GM's call.)

If the other party spies the villains first, they might stalk and ambush them, make a direct attack, or even parley depending on the circumstances and how tough the strangers appear.

GOOGLE IT!

When running *Necessary Evil: Breakout,* we highly recommend using Google Earth to "walk" the streets of New York and see the sights. Imagine your villains fighting in the streets filled with abandoned taxis and buses, or walking through the rubble of Grand Central Station where the v'sori bombarded it.

Remember also that besides the two separate alien attacks, the super-powered hero Iron Maiden went to town on the k'tharen champion Overbite. These two Cosmic-level beings toppled skyscrapers, threw buses, and created massive trenches in the city streets. Remember the fight with Zod in the film *Man of Steel?* That's the kind of damage these two titans caused, and none of it was cleaned up afterward.

Of course you can also *change* the streets of New York where you want. Need to add a particular monument, building, or park for one of your own Savage Tales? This is a different world, after all. And with a history of super heroes and villains the geography of the Big Apple might be significantly different than our own.

Still, there's a lot to be said for pulling out the laptop and showing your players what a walk down 5th Avenue looks like—at least before the v'sori destroyed it. This gives them a frame of reference, spawns new ideas for tactics, and generally immerses them more in the world. Throw in a group viewing of films like *Escape from New York* and the party should have a great idea of their surroundings.

ENCOUNTERS ABOVE

Whenever the villains take to the rooftops, the Game Master can use the table below to see if they encounter some other obstacle or denizen of the heights.

d20	Encounter
1–2	**Crumbling Rooftop:** The roof or roof ledge crumbles beneath 1d6 of the villains! Give each character an Agility roll at −2. Those who fail plummet 1d6 stories (d6+1 damage per story). Roll a die. If the result is odd, the group falls in on the lair of 3d6 Gangers (page 84).
3–8	**Buzzards:** A flock of 3d6 Buzzards is nearby. Roll a die. Even, Donald Bowers leads them. Make opposed Notice rolls for each group to see who spies who first. If the Buzzards win, they hide and wait until their prey is in a precarious position, then attack from ambush. Large or particularly dangerous-looking foes might be subject to a Push attack as they stand too near the edge! See Buzzards on page 81.
9–10	**K'lent's Blessing:** The v'sori Battle Master drops a crate of goods a few blocks away. See the **Cloudy With a Chance of Doom** Savage Tale on page 67.
11–16	**Gangers:** 4d6 Gangers (page 84) are on the rooftop. They might be keeping watch on their neighborhood from above, grilling some rare food they found, splitting up loot, or beating up prisoners from a rival gang.
17–18	**Vigilant Vigilantes:** Full Auto or Nevermore stalk the group from the rooftops. Either vigilante avoids a direct confrontation with targets who outnumber (and likely outclass) them, but might lure them into a gang or trap. Full Auto isn't above taking a sniper shot if he knows a villain is particularly deadly as well. See page 83 for Full Auto's statistics, and page 87 for Nevermore.
19–20	**Stash:** The villain finds an abandoned rooftop stash, unlooted apartment, or other cache. Treat this as Scavenging that takes only a few minutes. In addition to whatever valuables are found, the scavenger automatically finds 2d10 × $100 in dried foods, MREs, canned goods, and bottled beverages.

ABOVE

The skies and rooftops of the Big Apple are home to a gang called the Buzzards. V'sori patrols frequent the heights as well. These and random gangers or scavengers lurking along the skyline present a frequent threat to those villains who fly or swing through the city.

✦ **Safe At Last (79):** The villains are haunted by the ghost of a little girl with a very famous father. She might lead them to riches—or their doom!

V'SORI PATROLS

A trio of v'sori Battle Masters take turns patrolling the skies above the cordon in a mbuna transport. Inside the mbuna are the Battle Master's escorts, a half-dozen k'tharen armed to their very jagged teeth. The patrols have no set path—they roam wherever the Battle Master sees fit.

The patrol has orders to stay above the energy field, but one of the Battle Masters, K'lent, is a particularly cruel individual. He occasionally dips into the city to scatter a few treats—canned meat, soda, a six-pack of beer, and once even a sack full of cheeseburgers. Why? So he can watch the pitiful humans fight over them, of course.

Sh'tarka tolerates K'lent's indiscretions. The prison is an "ant farm," after all. See page 86 for k'tharen warrior statistics, and page 93 for the Battle Master.

✦ **Cloudy With a Chance of Doom (67):** The villains witness one of K'lent's drops and have a chance at a treat—or a trick!

THE BUZZARDS

Huntington Carver was a genius inventor who created numerous devices for the United States military. In the opening days of the original k'tharen invasion, he foolishly attempted to use some of his gizmos to fight the fins—and died a horrible and grisly death.

Carver's cache of weapons and other devices remained hidden in a basement for months before it was found by a canny survivor trying to flee from the Vermintide.

Donald Bowers was a thug with enough engineering knowledge to hire himself out to mad-scientist types. He even served as one of Dr. Destruction's minions once. When Bowers discovered Carver's stash he understood enough of the work to maintain it, if not create or design it himself.

Carver was about to ship his latest designs to the US Army testing facilities, so there was enough gear to outfit an army. Bowers did just that. He called himself the Buzzard, hired minions to serve *him* for a change, and started preying on New York City while its attention was still focused on the v'sori.

Like most everyone else, Bowers and his gang—the Buzzards—became trapped when Sh'tarka erected the cordon. He initially made a bid to control the streets and become the boss of New York, but a sound beating by Big Sis scared the crap out of him and the Buzzard retreated to the rooftops. He's now overly cautious and preys only on the weak.

BIRDS OF A FEATHER

The Buzzards wear high-tech stealth suits along with cybernetically linked wing apparatus. They also wear night-vision goggles and are armed with power claws that can tear through metal.

Fortunately, the Buzzards are otherwise normal thugs. Bowers taught them to be clever—to hit, fly, and stay out of reach of the hardened survivors of NYCP—but their strength and agility are on par with most other survivors.

The gang doesn't stay in one place for long. For protection, they move between dozens of aeries throughout the city. Most of these are well-stocked with goods stolen from the "grounders" below. Should a group find one of the Buzzards' lairs, multiply the value of any goods they find by 5.

See page 81 for a description of the Buzzard and his gang.

✦ **A Wing and a Scare (80):** The Buzzards dare to steal from the super villains!

"STICK TO THE ROOFTOPS. DON'T GET DRAWN INTO A FIGHT ON THE STREETS. YOU'LL LOSE."

—DONALD BOWERS

BELOW

The heights are dangerous and the streets are deadly, but below New York is pure hell.

There are scavs and gangers aplenty, but the number-one danger comes from the ravenous, ever-present Vermintide.

Despite that risk, dangers in the streets occasionally force scavengers into the old subway tunnels or even the sewers. Most think they have some special plan—a sealed-up or forgotten room or tunnel the Vermintide and other scavengers don't know about.

These unfortunate wretches might last a few days in such a place, but rats get in *everywhere,* and will eventually tip off the Vermintide that fresh food has delivered itself into their clutches.

THE VERMINTIDE

New York's underground is ruled by a terrible force of nature called the "Vermintide." At its core is a swarm of about a thousand black rats that escaped from a laboratory after the city-shaking battle between Iron Maiden and the k'tharen champion Overbite. The creatures fled into the sewer, mutated further, and over the next year developed the ability to attract, control, and shape *millions* of other rats.

Unfortunately for the prisoners of New York, the Vermintide's incessant hunger is growing out of control. It's devoured most everything (and everyone) it could find below ground and has begun erupting into the streets whenever its members smell fresh blood and manage to attract the attention of the core.

The Vermintide isn't omniscient and isn't in constant telepathic communication with every rat in the city, but it *can* do so when it exerts its considerable energies.

The Vermintide's statistics are found on page 91.

ENCOUNTERS BELOW

The depths of New York City are more dangerous than almost any other area.

d20	Encounter
1–4	**Crumbling Tunnels:** Whether the villains are in the sewers, subway, or the basement of a building looking for salvage, the damage caused by the alien invasion and the titanic battle between its super powered combatants has caused massive structural damage and it finally gives way. Each villain gets a Notice roll at −2 to hear the rumbling of debris or concrete from the street above about to fall. Those who make it get an Agility roll to get out of the way (the GM should add a +2 to +4 bonus to those with *speed* or similar powers as well). Those who fail suffer 4d6 damage from falling debris! Roll a die immediately after. If the result is odd, the Vermintide is attracted as well.
5–10	**Scavs:** A band of 4d6 scavengers have fled into the underground from some threat. If the villains fight them (blood is shed or loud noises/vibrations result), there's a 50% chance it attracts the Vermintide.
11–18	**Vermintide:** The patter of tiny feet turns into a thunderous rumble as two swarms of Vermintide race from the darkness and attack! If the swarms aren't defeated in four rounds, the central swarm is alerted! See the Vermintide, page 91.
19–20	**K'tharen Mutates:** 2d6 mutates stagger from the darkness. See page 86.

"THESE RATS WILL OUTLIVE US ALL. YOU, ME, TONY, SIS. PROBABLY EVEN NEUTRON."

—NEVERMORE

UPTOWN

Upper Manhattan is the closest thing the city has to sanctuary for the city's few remaining good-natured survivors. Villains had best beware though—the Harlem Knights don't take kindly to their type. Most of them are regular men and women, but there are a lot of them, they're well-led, and they stick together.

THE HARLEM KNIGHTS

Fireman Henry Jones is one of the few true heroes left in the city, but he's not a *super* hero. His gang of mostly ordinary men and women do their best to provide safety and refuge for those they deem good-natured and willing to pitch in.

They have a few gardens but aren't as self-sufficient as most believe. They horde ration bars when they can and gather and boil rainwater caught in rooftop cisterns to supplement their meager wares.

A number of super heroes and a few reformed villains fight for the Knights as well. See page 85 for the Knights' statistics.

NEVERMORE

Nevermore was once the Raven, sidekick to a caped crime fighter called the Owl. His mentor was driven mad by Phobos, the Master of Fear, then fell at the hands of a thug named Carlos Ragsdale.

Ragsdale's reputation soared after that and he was recruited by the mafia as one of their capos. Nevermore had a chance to escape New York before the cordon was activated, but he stayed to hunt Ragsdale. So far the coward has remained safely within the Red Hand compound where he constantly reminds everyone how he was the one who killed the infamous Owl.

Ragsdale knows Nevermore is after him—he barely escaped with his life on two separate occasions. He's offered a bounty on the hero, but the former sidekick is a tricky foe.

✦ **Bring Me the Head of Nevermore! (65):** Ragsdale grows increasingly paranoid and offers a large reward for Nevermore's head.

PHOBOS

The villain known as Phobos lives in the abandoned Hargrave Chemical Factory. The

UPTOWN ENCOUNTERS

This area is probably the safest for normal survivors in the entire NYCP. Of course, the player characters aren't normal survivors—they're villains. And the Harlem Knights hate bad guys!

d20	Encounter
1–2	**Vermintide:** Two swarms erupt from a storm drain, sewer opening, or manhole cover! The things are ravenous and attack till dispersed. See page 91.
3–4	**Chem Hounds:** A pack of 3d6 chem hounds (page 82) roaming in search of prey.
5–10	**Scavs:** A band of 3d6 scavengers (page 90) are spotted entering a building a few blocks away. They've found something of value. Multiple their normal loot by 3.
11–12	**Gangers:** 2d6 gangers stroll onto the Knights' turf looking for trouble. Roll a die. Odd, the gangers are Sykos.
13–15	**Harlem Knights:** A band of 2d6 knights accompanied by two super-powered protectors (any mix of those available to them) are out scavenging for supplies. They avoid trouble if possible, but fight a staged retreat back to their barricades if attacked.
16–18	**Heroes:** Blockbuster and Golden Gal stumble into the villains. Roll a die. Even, the dynamic duo decide the villains are a threat and come after them. Odd, they block the villains' path and warn them out of Uptown, but don't attack unless provoked. See page 81 and 84 for their statistics.
19–20	**K'tharen Mutates:** 1d6 mutates (page 86) emerge from an alley. They savagely attack the first thing they see.

compound is overrun by rabid chem hounds, of which even the Master of Fear is afraid. He's trapped there, out of his fear formula, and without friends.

✦ **The Essence of Fear (48):** This is part of the *Breakout!* Plot Point Campaign, but could be played separately. Dr. Phobos is out of ingredients for his fear formula. He wants more, and can share if the party helps him find what he needs.

MIDTOWN

The core of the Big Apple is rotten. Deadly and rotten. Big Sis and her Sykos rule the blood-soaked streets with mayhem and violence, and the Green Hag has taken over Central Park.

BIG SIS & THE SYKOS

Big Sis is chaotic, psychotic, and most other –otics one can think of. Her gang is really more of a cult of extreme hedonists. They do what they want, when they want, and to whom they want. They believe might makes right and if you can get away with it, there was nothing wrong with it in the first place.

Despite their extreme allegiance to anarchy, of course the Sykos have found a little order a bit more practical. They've taken up residence around Times Square, generally occupying the hotels and buildings from 8th to 5th Avenue and West 51st to West 29th. Big Sis has claimed Madame Tussauds and keeps it under constant guard. That's where she gets a lot of her wigs and costumes.

Sis is very canny, roaming the streets in disguise to keep tabs on her friends and enemies. She might dress as a gun moll and infiltrate Iron Head Tony's gang one day, dirty herself up and work the gardens with the Harlem Knights the next, then lead a violent "street march" of her Sykos as Big Sis after that.

There's a method to Big Sis' madness. Her goal is to keep the three major powers of the island—her Sykos, the Red Hand, and the Harlem Knights—relatively even. Why? Because she's afraid of *death*. She doesn't actually *kill* or order her people to since that might lead to some karmic revenge. She's violent and terrible, but she doesn't kill. When her Sykos capture foes, they are put through strange games and death traps instead of put to death. Those who die from chance, she believes, won't trigger the Grim Reaper's retaliation.

See Big Sis' profile for more about her strange phobia.

Sis' current office and abode is above the Majestic Theatre across the street from Madame Tussauds. The theater itself is mostly trashed, with scores of Sykos lounging or passed out among the seats. Her upstairs office is guarded 24/7 and looks like

MIDTOWN ENCOUNTERS

Big Sis' Sykos rule midtown and make up the vast majority of encounters here.

d20	Encounter
1–2	**Vermintide:** Two swarms erupt from a storm drain, sewer opening, or manhole cover! The things are ravenous and attack until dispersed.
3–4	**Sykos:** 3d6 Sykos rampage through the streets, setting cars on fire, smashing windows, and looking for trouble. Violent trouble.
5–10	**Syko Mob:** A mob of 20 Sykos stumble by, hyped upon a stash of booze or narcotics. They can't be reasoned with and attack anyone they see.
11–13	**Little Brother:** Big Sis' lieutenant ventures through the ruins looking for salvage—and trouble.
14–18	**Syko Army:** The Sykos are out in a force of around 50, and they're backed by at least two super-powered lieutenants. They might be partying or readying for a fight with a rival minor gang.
19–20	**K'tharen Mutates:** 2d6 mutates (page 86) emerge from an alley. They savagely attack the first thing they see. If the fight goes on for more than five rounds, 2d6 Sykos show up to pick off the survivors.

a hoarders' nightmare. She has hundreds of thousands of dollars' worth of goods, and piles and piles of absolute trash worth nothing to anyone in the prison.

See Big Sis and her gangers' profile on page 91.

✦ **Night Thing (73):** After defeating a band of Sykos, the villains are offered an opportunity to find a strange relic.

CENTRAL PARK

There's one area virtually everyone in New York avoids—Central Park. The once-beautiful island of green in the middle of the city has been taken over by a witch called the Green Hag. Trespassing in Central Park uses its own Encounter Table rather than the Midtown Encounters.

THE GREEN HAG

The park epitomizes the idea of "forbidden fruit." Literal fruit and other vegetables grow throughout the park in abundance. Strangely, the fruits grow on the *wrong* kinds of trees. Juicy red apples hang from oak branches while oranges grow on pines. Potatoes grow in dry earth and carrots, peas, and beans thrive in what used to be patches of grass or walkways.

Just as strange, the crops come and go daily. A patch of strawberries might be spotted beside a lemon tree one day, and the next there's nothing but grass and a dead oak.

The starving residents glare at the abundance daily, and there are always a few risk-takers willing to try a quick raid. Most of them—if they're quick and clever enough—can make it out of Central Park with a handful of fresh food. A few, however, are caught by tangling vines, wild dogs, or the witch's minions. Their fate is often far worse than starving to death.

Most of those caught "stealing" from the Green Hag are torn to shreds by the dogs or wolves, but some are held by masses of living vines till night falls—when the scarecrows come. These horrible servants of the witch carry the unfortunate soul away to some dark ritual—where they are transformed into more scarecrows in the Hag's service.

GRASPING VINES & FORBIDDEN FRUIT

The park is rife with fruit and vegetables, but they come and go in sporadic fashion.

CENTRAL PARK ENCOUNTERS

Use this table should the characters enter Central Park.

d20	Encounter
1–2	**The Green Hag:** The group spies a tree full of delectable fruit. They approach, and just as they are beginning to pick it feel a warm, fetid breeze from behind them. The fruit blackens and dies in their hands…then the horrible figure of the Green Hag appears! Roll a die. Odd, her dogs are with her. Even, Aileen the Burner is by her side. See page 85.
3–4	**Release the Hounds:** The Green Hag's dogs (page 85) appear from the foliage—and protect their master's property.
5–10	**Trespassers:** A band of 2d6 scavs (page 90) desperate for fruit has found a seemingly unguarded tree. They've gathered 2d6 × $100 in fruit (NYCP value) and are about to leave when discovered. Defeating the scavs won't be hard, but any loud noise (gunshot, blaster-type power, yelling, etc.) draws the Green Hag's dogs (see **Release the Hounds**, above).
11–13	**Gangers:** As **Trespassers,** above, but the intruders are gangers instead (page 84). Roll a die. Odd, the gangers are Sykos.
14–18	**Aileen the Burner:** The Green Hag's faithful servant has detected the villains' presence. He summons the hounds as backup, approaches the group, and tells them to leave immediately. If they don't, he sics the hounds on them and follows up with his own attacks.
19	**Lucky Day:** A tree full of fresh ripe fruit stands unguarded. The villains can gather several baskets of it before another encounter must be generated. Each villain picking rolls a d6 (which can Ace). Add all the rolls together and multiply by $100 to get the combined value of the haul (at NYCP prices).
20	**Vines:** The villains find fresh fruits and vegetables (as **Lucky Day**, above) but are attacked by legions of grasping vines and limbs! These act as swarms, and there is one per raider. The swarms cause damage as usual, but also grapple. (See **Swarm** in *Savage Worlds*.)

Finding a stash of food requires an hour and a Notice roll at −4 (not Survival—the park makes no logical sense). Make this a Group roll if the villains scour the park together.

Failure means the group finds 1d10 × $10 worth of fruits and vegetables but generates an encounter.

Success means the seeker finds 1d10 × $100 worth of fruits and vegetables and generates an encounter.

A raise is the same as a success but generates no encounter with the Green Hag or her minions.

✦ **Scurvy Dogs (76):** Even villains have friends, and one of them needs vitamin C ASAP. The fruit in Central Park is ripe and juicy.

THE FIXER

Big Sis grants protection to a few skilled individuals within her domain. One of them is the Fixer. The elderly lady was once a super villain named Miss Mechanical who enjoyed a long career robbing banks, creating killer robots, and hiring out her services to other super villains to destroy their foes with.

Now in her 60s, the Fixer no longer ventures out to do battle herself. Instead, she repairs technology for Big Sis and her various minions in exchange for food, shelter, and protection.

The Fixer has a weak spot for cats. Her lab in the basement of Madame Tussauds is crawling with them. It is the one place the Vermintide fears, as well. The thing could easily overwhelm the felines, but its rat brain smells the pheromones and gives it a wide berth. The Fixer's statistics are on page 83.

DOWNTOWN ENCOUNTERS

The Red Hand doesn't tolerate any nonsense around the Chelsea Piers area. If they see trouble, Iron Hand Tony's men close up the barricades, arm themselves to the teeth, and start firing. They'll ask questions later. The docks and wharves in the rest of the Lower Manhattan are fair game, however.

d20	Encounter
1–2	**Vermintide:** Two swarms erupt from a storm drain, sewer opening, manhole cover, or wharf! The things are ravenous and attack until dispersed.
3–4	**Chem Hounds:** A wild pack of 3d6 chem hounds roam the street looking for prey.
5–6	**Scavs:** 1d6 scavengers push shopping carts and wheelbarrows through the street. The carts are loaded with paltry goods to sell to the Red Hand. Triple the normal loot for scavengers (page 90).
7–10	**Gangers:** 2d6 gangers sneak through downtown looking to waylay scavengers bringing loot to Iron Head Tony. Their statistics are on page 84.
12–14	**Vigilant Vigilantes:** Full Auto or Nevermore stalk the group from the rooftops. Either vigilante avoids a direct confrontation with targets who outnumber (and likely outclass) them, but might lure them into a gang or trap. Full Auto isn't above taking a sniper shot if he knows a villain is particularly deadly as well. See page 83 for Full Auto's statistics, and page 87 for Nevermore.
15–18	**Heroes:** Blockbuster and Golden Gal stumble onto the villains. Roll a die. Even, the dynamic duo decide the villains are a threat and come after them. Odd, they block the villains' path and warn them out of Uptown, but don't attack unless provoked. See pages 81 and 84 for their statistics.
19	**Convoy:** 1d6 cars and trucks move through the streets from midtown to the Red Hand compound. They're loaded with goods (2d6 × $5,000 worth) and protected by 20 members of the Red Hand (page 89), four enforcers (page 89), and three super beings.
20	**K'tharen Mutates:** 1d6 mutates (page 86) emerge from an alley. They savagely attack the first thing they see.

DOWNTOWN

The piers, warehouses, and buildings on the lower western end of the island are well-kept and occupied by the Red Hand and their hundreds of hangers-on.

The southern and eastern dockside areas are in much worse shape. Squatters hide within the concrete buildings and the piers have already begun to rot without the city's continual maintenance. The v'sori sank all the boats of significant size. Some of their shattered hulls bash rhythmically against the docks, clinging to their moorings by frayed ropes with the constant tide.

✦ **Gang War (68):** When most of the villains reach Heroic level, a savage Gang War begins!

THE RED HAND

The Red Hand holds a collection of buildings along the Western waterfront, including what was once the Chelsea Piers mall. A barricade runs along West Street, guarded by blaster nests and over a dozen guards. Entrance is easy for customers though—the Red Hand is open for trade 24/7. The compound has hundreds of people there at all times, buying, selling, begging, and socializing like it's the end of the world.

The leader of the Red Hand is Iron Head Tony. His remaining "family" members are the senior staff. Other survivors who have proven themselves to him serve as the second ring of guards and gratefully receive extra rations for doing so.

Wives, girlfriends, and serving staff live in the houses and apartments on West 24th through 17th Streets. The rest of the people here are transients from other parts of the city. Most are civilians looking for as much comfort and normalcy as possible, some are revelers enjoying their relative freedom, and others are a constant chain of scavengers bringing in everything from cans of soup to priceless works of art.

✦ **Let 'Em Eat Cannoli (72):** K'lent drops a particularly desirable treat into the city and Iron Head Tony wants it. Now.

IRON HEAD TONY'S BIG PLAN

For now, Iron Hand Tony is content to hoard resources and sell them at a steady and vigorous profit in other goods. But he has a much bigger plan. The Red Hand allows all sorts of vices within their section of the city—drugs, prostitution, gambling, and anything else that doesn't negatively affect their business is all fair game. One of the more lucrative vices has proven to be arena battles.

The first fights were between brawny champions or desperate souls looking for a decent meal or much-needed medicine. But a few of the brawls took place between low-level supers. They proved popular and Tony's bookies made a tidy profit on them. More importantly, Tony noticed the occasional v'sori patrol hovering overhead. The aliens *enjoyed* the show.

That's when Tony got his "Big Idea." His pet hacker, Emil Voga, otherwise known as Byte, placed a transmitter on top of the Red Hand warehouse. It broadcasts the fights to the v'sori along with a private, encoded message telling the aliens Tony can stage the fights professionally and broadcast them to the world if they'll just open up regular, controlled entry to New York City.

Like the ancient Romans, Tony says, these "bread and circuses" will appease the conquered masses, help quell the resistance, and of course…make Tony a very, very rich man. He calls the proposed show "*ARENA!*", and knows if he can just get the v'sori's cooperation it'll be the biggest thing since the invasion.

Of course, Tony has also been hoarding cash, art objects, and other valuables scavenged from NYC in hopes the aliens will allow him and his show staff to move back and forth through the cordon. Combined with his take on *ARENA!*, he'll be rich as Midas.

✦ **Arena! (55):** A fight between Big Sis and the villains is the culmination of one of the *Breakout!* Plot Points..

BREAKOUT!

Breakout! is the story of the New York City Prison and the player character villains' attempt to escape it.

Things within the cordon are getting desperate. Decent food and clean water are firmly controlled by the Red Hand, medicine dried up long ago, the nights are long and dark, and bullets are the new currency. The city is controlled by a number of major gangs and dozens of smaller ones.

A massive, sentient swarm of rats grow uncontrolled in the sewers, the murderous Buzzards stalk the heights, the mad Sykos control the streets, and frenzied, mutated k'tharen occasionally erupt from some unknown locale.

The player characters are street level villains trying to survive on these mean streets. Fortunately for them, they're about to be shown a way out. It's not an easy way out, and it will take some time…but those who survive will escape the v'sori cordon and break out of the hell hole that is the New York City Prison. They might even help Dr. Destruction's resistance, whether they intend to or not.

CAMPAIGN SUMMARY

Here are the major beats of the story, which should be interspersed with Savage Tales from this book or of your own creation.

Easy Pickings: The villains bond over some violence and mayhem. Afterwards, they meet Firefly, a villain sent into the prison to deliver a message from Dr. Destruction. If they gather a certain set of items, he promises, they will be shown a way out of the prison.

The Essence of Fear: One of the ingredients the team must gather is Dr. Phobos' fear formula. They find the super villain at the Hargrave Chemical Factory and he reveals the items he needs to complete their request.

Deep Dive: The villains break into an office building and battle killer robots to retrieve a set of experimental deep diving suits.

The Mistress of Mayhem: One of Dr. Destruction's items is a charm bracelet worn by the titania of terror, Big Sis. She doesn't come out to play easily though, so the villains must wage war against her psychotic minions to draw her out.

Deals With Devils: The party requires a map in the possession of the Red Hand. Iron Head Tony demands a half a *million* dollars in goods, kicking off a dangerous scavenger hunt through the city.

Arena!: Big Sis eventually comes out of hiding, but will only fight the villains at the Red Hand's televised gladiatorial show—*ARENA!*

Escape From New York: Finally, all the ingredients assembled, Firefly delivers Dr. Destruction's final message. The group must descend below the subway, below the sewers, and into an old, secret Nazi submarine pen. There they find the source of the k'tharen mutates plaguing the city, uncover a secret v'sori plan, and—if they survive—escape the New York City Prison.

EASY PICKINGS

It's nearly two months after the cordon was erected on May 15th, 2002. The villains all know each other and have been surviving together for at least a few weeks. Some of them might have worked for other gangs and had a falling out, some might have worked for other groups that were destroyed in recent gang wars, and some might be loners who finally decided they needed at least a few occasional companions to survive. *Let the players decide why their characters are with the group.* Their villains don't have to *like* the other miscreants, but they have decided to work with them—at least for a while.

Once the group has figured out why they're together, it's time for a little violence and destruction. The tale begins as the group hear sounds of gunfire from a nearby street. Gunfire has become rare as bullets become scarce so it definitely attracts their attention.

A block away, the group comes upon a familiar scene—a band of unaffiliated scavs is attacking another band of scavs over a makeshift cart filled with food and other goodies. The player characters are definitely tougher than these mooks so they should charge in, bash some heads, and take the loot for themselves. The moment they do, both groups of scavs decide to settle their differences later. They turn on the intruders and fight until more than half of them are Incapacitated or worse.

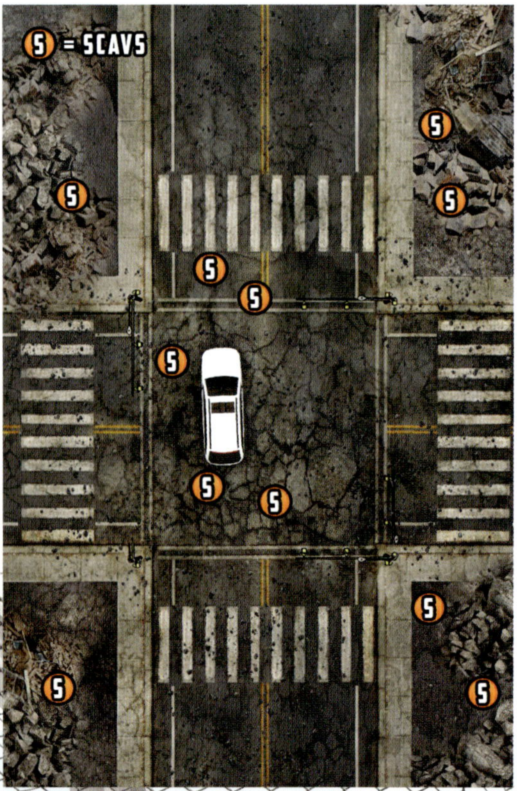

Game Masters, this is a chance for your villains to feel powerful and tough right from the start. The scavs attack with everything they've got but should be chumps compared to the player characters.

- **Scav Defenders (11):** Use the scav profile found on page 90. Six of the scavs were originally attacking the other five, but they've banded together to fight their common foe for now.

LOOT

Inside the cart is a decent haul of ammo, batteries, canned goods, a few water bottles, and some jewelry. All together, the stuff is worth $500.

MESSENGER OF DESTRUCTION

As soon as the villains have recovered the goods, a flying figure lands among them. This is Firefly, a well-known gadgeteer who uses fire-based weapons. He has a thick New York accent and is very familiar with the area, but only from before the war. His costume is a dark orange jumpsuit, helmet with flame pattern, flamethrower, and a silver jump pack.

> *"Woah, woah, woah, friends! I come in peace! I swear on my flamethrower! Hey, nice haul you got there…can I have summa that?"*

Regardless of the answer, Firefly looks all around as if wary of other eyes and ears and suggests they move someplace private. He says he has a message for them…from the *outside.*

> *"I've only been here a few days. Been looking for you ever since. Yeah…the aliens are still dumping people into New York, but no one's coming out. Not yet, anyway. That's what I'm here to talk to you guys about.*
>
> *"See, there's a resistance movement out there. It's called Omega. We're givin' it to 'em good in Star City…for some reason the v'sori ain't leveled the place yet…but Omega is worldwide. Wanna know who*

leads it? Our ol' pal, Dr. Destruction… that's who."

Firefly lets that sink in for a moment.

"I don't know why, exactly, but Dr. Destruction wants your group—we call it a 'cell'—to break out. So I hadda get captured and thrown in here so I could tell you how. I'm uh…I'm hopin' you'll take me witcha when the time comes."

Firefly hands the character with the highest Charisma (or whoever seems like the leader) a small metal disc two inches in diameter and a half-inch thick. The villains should be familiar with these—it's a holoslug. When placed in a holoplayer (which they likely don't have yet—see below), it plays a prerecorded holographic message.

Either way, Firefly doesn't stick around.

"Don't play it now. I don't wanna see it. DD was very specific that this is for your eyes only. I got a commlink here for ya that'll reach me. I'm gonna find some ration bars, hole up somewhere high, and wait this thing out. We don't have a lotta spare batteries so I'll check in at high noon every day. Got it? Need somethin', I'll do my best, but I ain't quite in the same league as you guys so I'm stayin' outta the way. But when you're ready to bolt, say the word and I'll come in hot."

Unless anyone has any questions, Firefly takes off. He can answer any other basic inquiries about the invasion or how life is going outside the cordon, but he doesn't know anything else about their mission.

A FEW PILES OF GARBAGE LATER…

Finding a holoplayer and batteries might take a little poking around. Use the Scavenging rules on page 18 to do so.

When the holoslug is played, Dr. Destruction's imposing figure springs to life and delivers the following message. Start by addressing the "leader" of the group or whoever has the highest Charisma by name wherever it says (Leader) in the dialogue below:

"Greetings (Leader). I'm glad to hear you survived the v'sori cordon of New York City. I'm sure you'd like to escape and join the rest of us in freeing our planet from these alien scum…and I have devised a way for you to do so. You and any companions you've acquired.

"To escape from New York you will need to gather some items. It you follow my directions precisely the plan has a 93.7% chance of success. You have up to six months to complete these tasks. Not a day longer. Write this down or memorize the list—this message will irrevocably delete itself five minutes after activation."

At that the image of Dr. Destruction's face vanishes and a wall of text appears, revealing the following list:

- 100 gallons of Phobos' fear formula in *liquid* form.
- Ultraviolet (UV) goggles or lamp (a black light) to see "invisible" paint.
- Big Sis' charm necklace.
- A specially-marked map of the New York City underground from the Red Hand.

- Experimental deep diver suits for all your team who require oxygen to breathe. You'll find what you need at the offices of Russell Engineering. You'll know when to use them, but before you do, make sure to disperse the fear formula ahead of you. Then follow directly behind it.

Collecting these items will take some time but that's okay—the villains have six months before Warlord Sh'tarka's plans are ready, which is what Dr. Destruction is trying to stop. This should give you plenty of time to run the Plot Point Campaign, numerous Savage Tales, and any adventures or side-quests of your own creation.

SCAVENGER HUNT

Below is a list of the items and where they can be found, most of which result in Savage Tales. Exactly how the cell gathers these ingredients and in what order is up to them.

- **Phobos' Fear Formula:** The Essence of Fear, page 48. Once cornered, Phobos reveals he needs more ingredients, some of which can be found via Scavenging (page 18), and others that result in the Savage Tales **Neutron** (75) or **The Ice Queen** (72), and **This is Your Brain on Fear** (76).
- **UV Goggles/Lamp:** The group should use the Scavenging rules on page 18 to find this necessity, or simply buy it from the Red Hand for $100.
- **Big Sis' Charm Necklace:** The Mistress of Mayhem, page 53.
- **Map of the Underground:** Deals with Devils, page 54. This kicks off a quest for a half-million in goods that must be acquired through scavenging or other adventures.
- **Deep Diver Suits:** Deep Dive, page 51.

THE ESSENCE OF FEAR

Item: 100 gallons of Phobos' fear formula.

Dr. Phobos is an extortionist. He poisons his targets with drugs, gas, and other chemicals, then exploits his victims' terror for whatever nefarious purpose suits his current goals. He's caused city-wide panic on multiple occasions, and has made more than a few heroes question their own sanity.

The doctor was also responsible for the death of the Owl, once the city's most feared caped crusader. Dr. Phobos poisoned him so drastically the experienced crime fighter was killed by a low-level hoodlum named Carlos Ragsdale. See the Savage Tale **Bring Me the Head of Nevermore!** (65) for the gory details.

Dr. Phobos was very active immediately after the cordon, using his gas to send neighboring gangs into fear-filled violence against their own members while he consolidated control of his own people. But that was in the beginning…no one can recall hearing anything about him in the last few months.

With a Streetwise roll and a little time spent talking to other survivors, the team learns that before his disappearance, Dr. Phobos was occasionally seen northwest of Harlem. With a raise, a former goon says he was a minion for Phobos for a couple weeks a few years back, and that he kept a base in the long abandoned Hargrave Chemical Factory. Without a raise, the villains must canvas the general area for a day. Generate an additional encounter, and when it's over, they run into the same goon and get the information they need.

The minion, Max Klieber, doesn't know much else about the doc. He kept to himself and only shared what he needed to with his minions. Max says there's a lab inside the factory somewhere, but he never saw it. He and the others only showed up for jobs when the master summoned them.

- **Dr. Phobos:** See page 83.

THE HARGRAVE CHEMICAL FACTORY

Doctor Phobos used one of the regular research labs in the old office buildings, but keeps a private lair hidden deeper in a converted storage bunker. Phobos has no minions at this time—he has no way to pay them and is out of the chemicals he needs to manufacture his trademark formula or any of its variants. He has a few existing bombs and booby traps left, but not enough of the raw formula for any substantial plan.

Phobos is actually somewhat trapped at the present...a large pack of slavering dogs have gotten into the toxins pooled around the site and taken up residence. They attack anything that enters their territory.

- **Chem Hounds (3+1/Villain):** Packs of vicious, mutated canines prowl the Hargrave Chemical Factory. See page 82.

PRIMAL FEARS

Dr. Phobos watches the fight between the intruders and the chem hounds from a ruined gantry overlooking the main grounds. He doesn't know what the villains want and figures he's better safe than sorry.

As soon as the last chem hound is defeated, Phobos triggers one of his last reserves of fear chemical...an odorless mist that strikes at the intruders' most basic, instinctual fears. Read the following as the villains finish off the last of the canines:

You dispatch the last baying hound. For a moment, you hear nothing but your teammates' panting. Then something moves on the ruined walls surrounding you... something large that clacks on the concrete as it approaches. You look up and see hairy, insectoid arms reaching over the walls. Giant spiders!

Then something else fades into view behind the wall...the massive figure of Dr. Phobos! He wears his trademark long coat, fedora, and dark glasses...but is almost 50 feet tall! He laughs loudly, nearly shattering your eardrums...as the giant spiders descend and attack!

The giant Dr. Phobos and spiders are illusions, of course, but under the effects of the formula they're real enough to kill their victims. The gas lasts 10 combat rounds, after which time all the figures dissolve into mist. Even if the *players* figure out the trick, the chemical is too strong for the *characters* to ignore, so "disbelieving" has no effect—but points for trying!

Dr. Phobos doesn't attack, but on the first round of the fight and any round in which he's dealt a red Action Card, he laughs in a massive booming voice. The heroes must make Vigor rolls at −2 or be Shaken!

PHANTASMAL SPIDERS

There's one spider per villain, and they only go after one opponent each. The creatures only gang up if a victim is down.

The villains *can* flee. The spiders give chase at the speed of their prey, but that suits Dr. Phobos just fine as long as the potential enemies leave his lair.

Attributes: Agility d10, Smarts d6 (A), Spirit d10, Strength Special, Vigor d10
Skills: Fighting d12, Notice d10, Stealth d12

Pace: See below; **Parry:** 8; **Toughness:** 11(4)
Special Abilities
- **Armor +4:** Chitinous carapace.
- **Bite/Claw:** Str+d8.
- **Improved Frenzy:** The spiders attack with a bite or fast stab with their spiked legs.
- **Pace:** The spiders have the same Pace as the foe they're chasing, plus 1!
- **Phantasmal Damage:** Any damage the things cause is calculated normally but is actual purely mental. Once the spiders fade, damage also fades at the rate of one wound every minute. If someone is Incapacitated, they're simply unconscious for 1d6 × 10 minutes.
- **Strength:** The spiders have the same Strength as the current foe they're attacking. It changes instantly should the thing attack a target with different strength.

CHEMISTRY 1001

A character with Phobos' notes, the ingredients, and Knowledge (Chemistry) might also brew the formula. It's a tricky process, especially given the nature of the equipment, spotty power (if a generator can be found), and less than ideal conditions, so the total penalty is −8. Each batch must also brew for 24 hours.

If the roll is successful, the fear formula is made in liquid form. (Which is what Dr. Destruction told the group to create.)

Failure ruins the batch and consumes all the ingredients *except* the uranium or plutonium. Those isotopes are good for hundreds of uses.

WEAPONIZED FEAR

There's enough of the formula left over to make 2d6 gas grenades. Phobos wants these for himself, but if double-crossed, commanded, cajoled, or bribed, he'll hand them over to the party.

Gas grenades are thrown just like normal frag grenades, but everyone within the area of effect must make a Fear test at −4. Extras who make the roll suffer −2 to Trait rolls for the next 10 rounds, and Panic for 10 rounds if they fail. Wild Cards suffer −2 to Trait rolls for 10 rounds if they succeed, and roll on the Fear Table at +4 if they fail.

EXTERMINATED

Once the villains have overcome the spiders and confronted Dr. Phobos, he tries to play up the fact that they saved him from the chem hounds. Phobos figures that if he appears grateful and offers them payment (he has $400 worth of canned goods and drinks stashed in his lab), he'll be better off than letting them set the tone of the encounter. If that doesn't work and the villains threaten him for the formula, Phobos offers the same terms set out below but in a different tenor.

Either way, Dr. Phobos speaks in a low, sibilant whisper:

> *"You want…my formula? 100 gallons? Goodness me. That is a lot. I would gladly share it with friends such as you. But I'm afraid some of the raw materials have run out many weeks ago. I have nothing but a few personal gadgets left…nowhere near enough for the volume you require."*

When pressed for the location of the raw materials, Phobos continues.

> *"You want the most potent version of the formula, I suppose. Far more terrible than that I…mistakenly…affected you with. These things are most difficult to find, of course, given the state of the city, but I'll make a deal with you. I'll tell you where you might find all you need and then some, and I'll brew it for you—which takes great skill and considerable practice. But you leave me the extra. I would like to return to my former…status…"*

The doctor can't gather the ingredients himself. Without his formula he's fairly powerless.

Deal or no deal, Phobos eventually presents the following list:

- **10 pounds sodium nitrite:** This kind of salt is used for curing meat and might be found at specialty supermarkets throughout the city. Use the **Scavenging** rules on page 18. Each Necessity can be used to find one pound of sodium nitrite. Up to 1d6+2 pounds can also be purchased from the Red Hand for $1,000 per pound—it's very rare and few know what it is so very little has been traded. (The Red Hand pays only $250 per pound for it since so few know what to do with it.)

- **8 ounces of uranium or plutonium:** There were no nuclear containment facilities within the cordon that Phobos knows of, but he knows of two other sources. One is the power core for a robotic villain called Neutron. The robot disappeared during the battle between OverBite and Iron Maiden and hasn't been seen since. The other source is the Ice Queen's freeze ray gun. Not so long ago, the hero known as Nevermore froze one of his enemies and shattered them into ice cubes. It's very possible he has her gun. See the Savage Tales **Neutron** (page 75) or **The Ice Queen** (page 72) should the group seek them out.
- **Synthesized norepinephrine:** This very rare, experimental drug is an artificial version of the natural chemical formed in the human brain. Dr. Phobos tells the group they are likely to find some in the laboratory of the Malidore Institute for Advanced Sleep Studies in uptown. "Get as much as you can," he offers. He doesn't say how he knows the extract will be there, but might admit to "farming" it from volunteers there if pressed. See the Savage Tale **This is Your Brain on Fear** (page 76).

CREATING THE FORMULA

The sodium nitrite is used as a catalyst while the radioactive material alters the norepinephrine at the quantum level. Norepinephrine is the chemical produced by the brain to trigger one's flight or fight response. Trust us. It's science!

Brewing the actual fear from the components is a tricky process that requires Phobos himself and about four hours.

It's unlikely the villains can mix the ingredients themselves, but see the **Chemistry 1001** sidebar. Should something happen to Dr. Phobos, they'll have to find his notes in the bowels of the factory and give it a try. They might also find another "mad scientist" (like the Fixer) to give it a try if they can be convinced to do so.

The final result is 100 gallons—give or take—of liquefied terror. Phobos delivers it in two 55-gallon metal drums. Each drum weighs around 450 pounds fully loaded, so moving them requires a hand truck or dolly, or a character with super strength.

Phobos also provides an aluminum wrench for opening the barrels.

> *"Be very careful with that," the Master of Fear says as you take possession of the barrels. "It is my life's work, you know. I hope this is either for a very large creature or dozens of smaller ones. Increased doses rarely have any effect on a single target. I was...fortunate once...with the Owl, but that was an unfor...er, fortunate outlier."*

DEEP DIVE

Item: Experimental deep diving suits.

A design company called Russell Engineering was working on new prototype suits for the US Navy when the invasion occurred. They remain in the company's sealed storage vault in lower Manhattan awaiting better days. Finding the company requires either a few hours talking to people and a Streetwise roll at −2, or scrounging up an actual, intact print copy of the Yellow Pages that hasn't been used for fuel or toilet paper, a Survival (Urban) roll at −2 and 1d6 hours of looking.

Russell Engineering is located on the eastern end of 84th Street on Gracie Square, right by the water. It's locked up tight with blast doors strong enough to keep out all the local scavengers so far. The heavy steel doors are Toughness 16. If the villains can't manage that, they can scavenge up a high-powered blowtorch using the **Scavenging** rules for Necessities on page 18. It can also be bought from the Red Hand for $1,000—though they will absolutely follow the group to see what's so valuable.

The team might also try the roof (it's a single-story building). A pack of Buzzards is perched on the adjacent building though (four stories high), so the characters might be ambushed first. If the Buzzards are driven off or defeated, the group finds a skylight they can use to get inside.

- **Buzzards (2 per villain):** See page 82.

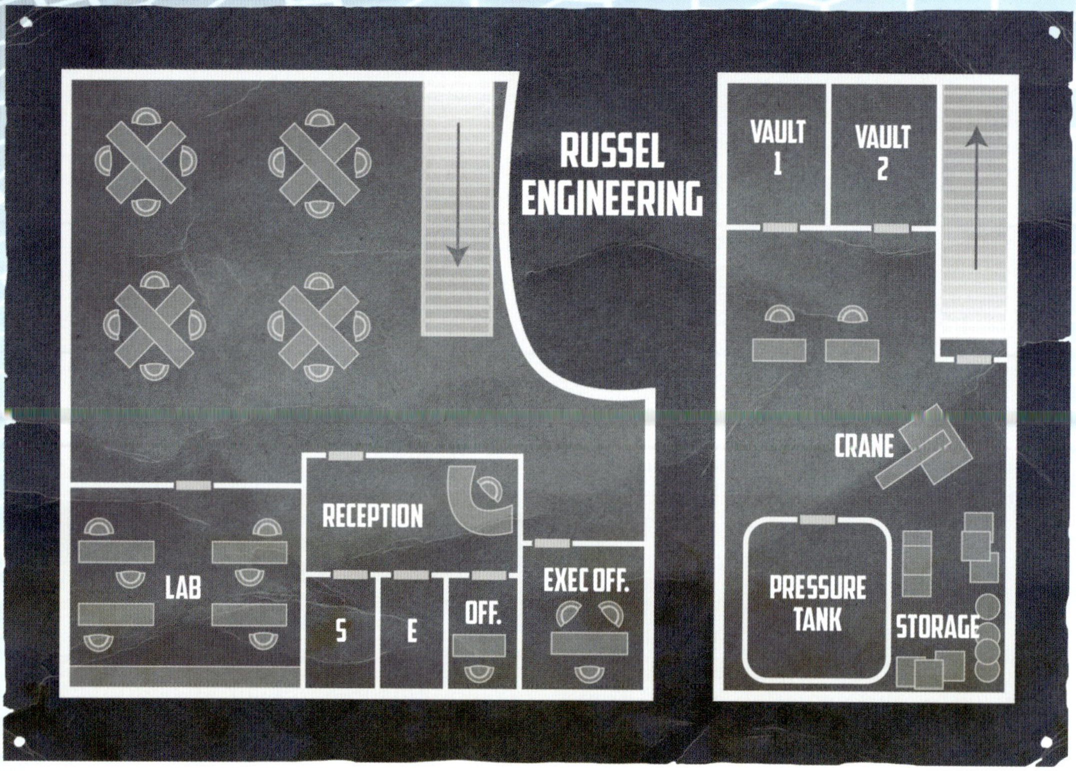

RUSSELL ENGINEERING LAB

The main floor of the building is half office and half lab. A curved reception desk greets anyone who comes through the door, while the skylight drops the villains in directly over the star-cluster work stations in front of the glass tech lab.

The lab seems to have been locked up tight and left in good order. The blast doors were locked electronically, as were the interior metal window shutters.

But that's not the building's only security.

KILLER ROBOTS, OF COURSE

The main problem with investigating an engineering firm is that they make things—like killer robots to protect their designs!

When the villains enter, red emergency lights flicker to life—but nothing else happens. Yet.

The door to the basement is locked and takes either Lockpicking at −4 to open or it can be broken down (Toughness 8). When the group descends, sentry bots rise up out of the darkness, scan the intruders for one round barking "HALT AND SHOW IDENTIFICATION," then attack on the next.

- **Sentry Bots (6):** See below.

RUSSELL ENGINEERING SENTRY BOTS

The sentries are fast-moving, flying drones. They're spherical balls with a single, red eye bouncing back and forth in a black eye slit. They're propelled by hover fans and equipped with another of Russell Engineering's inventions—a powerful stun ray. Unfortunately for the characters, the drones' testing was never finished. They continue to stun their victims even after they're down—eventually causing the target's heart to stop if allowed to continue!

Attributes: Agility d10, Smarts d4, Spirit d10, Strength d4, Vigor d10

Skills: Notice d8, Shooting d12

Pace: 48; **Parry:** 2; **Toughness:** 9 (4)

Special Abilities:

- **Armor +4:** The drones are encased in thin titanium.
- **Construct:** +2 to recover from being Shaken, doesn't breathe, ignores one level of wounds, immune to poison and disease.
- **Flight:** Pace 48, −2 to hit. Climb 3.
- **Self-Destruct:** Russell Engineering was paranoid their designs would fall into their rivals' hands. When a drone is destroyed, it blows up in a Medium Burst Template for 3d10 damage.

• **Size −2:** The drones are roughly the size of basketballs.

• **Small:** Attackers subtract 2 from their from their attack rolls to hit.

• **Stun Ray:** The sentry bots are equipped with integral mega-tasers (see page 14). If a target is hit while already stunned from the taser (and he is a living being with a human heart), failing the Vigor roll causes a heart attack! See the **Fright Table** in *Savage Worlds* for the grisly results.

THE SUITS

Once the bots are destroyed, the group can pilfer the vaults. Vault One contains the experimental suits. There are a dozen here so they should have enough for themselves plus any sidekicks or minions.

Each suit has eight hours of oxygen in an extraordinarily small tank about the size of an aerosol can.

Vault Two contains several prototype inventions that can be pilfered:

• **Night Vision Contacts:** These contact lenses are made of a special breathable material that never has to be changed or replaced. Though they are a device, since they can't usually be taken away, the Device modifier is not incurred. The contacts give the wearer *heightened senses (Low Light Vision).*

• **Nega Bomb:** Designed to take out supers, these three "bombs" are triggered by accompanying remotes. When the remote detonator is pressed (a free action), the bomb explodes in a Large Burst Template. Every super-powered being in the burst radius loses their powers for 1d6 rounds (roll for each individual).

• **Power Harness:** A lightweight strength enhancer that runs under the arms, back and legs. It grants the wearer *super attribute: Strength +1, Device.*

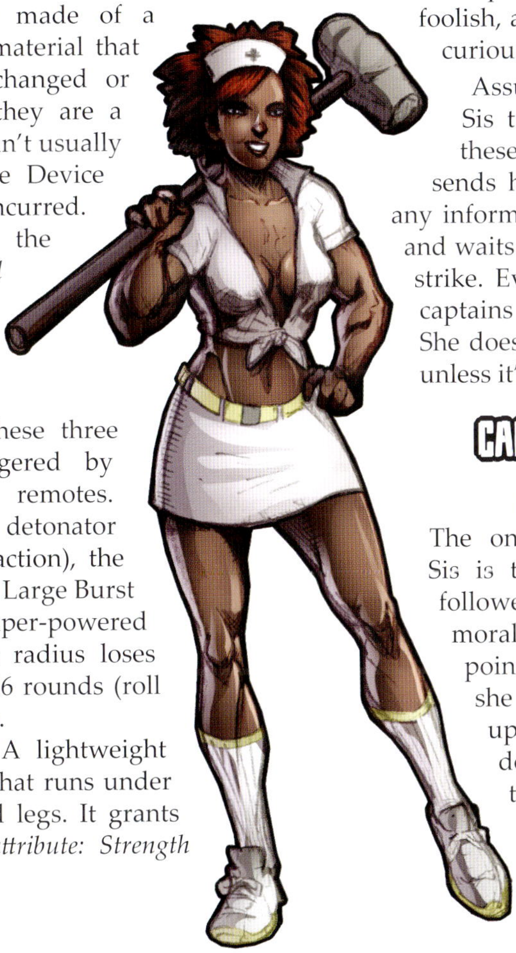

THE MISTRESS OF MAYHEM!

Item: Big Sis' charm necklace.

Big Sis is perhaps the most elusive of the party's targets and likely the most dangerous. Waltzing into her domain is ill-advised. There are about 3,000 of her demented followers there, including several dozen with super powers.

The best plan for getting to Big Sis is to draw her out. This takes a while, but is likely the only way to corner the cagey mistress.

If the team wants to try the direct approach and challenge Big Sis on her home turf, several hundred Sykos respond instead, and a dozen captains join in 1d4 rounds later.

Sis watches from a distant vantage point. She doesn't attack, but instead allows her horde to swarm over the intruders and tear them to pieces. She's mad but not foolish, and as cautious as she is curious.

Assuming anyone lives, Sis tries to figure out what these fools were after. She sends her Sykos out to gather any information on them they can and waits for the right moment to strike. Even then, she sends her captains to do the dirty work. She doesn't care to fight anyone unless it's on her terms.

CAN SIS COME OUT AND PLAY?

The only way to get to Big Sis is to whittle away at her followers. Eventually, their morale disintegrates to the point where she must prove she isn't afraid of these upstarts. If the players don't figure this out for themselves, prod them a bit—as villains this is something that would occur to them naturally after a time.

SNEAKS & THIEVES

It's possible the villains have a character who can short-circuit the adventure by somehow getting to Big Sis and simply lifting her charm necklace. Sis is clever enough to plan accordingly if she knows what's coming, but if the villains are extremely clever, it's not necessary to completely deny their victory.

If the necklace is taken and Big Sis knows who did it, she challenges them to the match in **Arena!** (page 55) and things progress similarly to the events described there. If she doesn't know who did it, she starts trying to find out, and assuming any possible way to do so, she does, then again challenges them to the *ARENA!* match. In essence, try your best to make the *ARENA!* match happen, but try not to take away the players' agency when doing so.

Each time the group battles Sis' Sykos, rate the fight from 0 to 3 based on the scale below:

DRAWING OUT BIG SIS

Rating	Encounter Results
0	A few Sykos are defeated outside Midtown.
1	A few Sykos are defeated in or near Midtown, or the battle takes place farther away but the player characters are particularly nasty to them.
2	A large group of Sykos are defeated including at least one lieutenant, and the player characters make a big impression on them somehow.
3	The villains do something big, bold, and obvious to the Sykos.

HIT TEAMS

Once the group accumulates three points worth of incidents, Sis sends out hit teams to take care of them. The hit teams aren't competent enough to find the group's lair if they have one, but whenever the villains are out and about, there's a 50% chance the hit team strikes.

Consider the timing carefully. They might stalk the group and attack while they're involved with some other threat, or they might simply run into the villains on their way to or from some other destination. The team consists of 10 Sykos and one captain for every two player characters.

If the villains' lair is well-known, three hit teams strike at once. Best of luck to the tainted but brave souls.

BIG SIS TAKES NOTICE

Once the tally hits 10, Big Sis can no longer ignore the challenge to her authority. Her minions spread the word all over town… their boss and her chosen champions challenge the villains to a death match. Soon after, Iron Head Tony contacts Big Sis. This is the kind of event he's been waiting for to kick off his new pit-fighting gladiator show (which he thinks will win him special consideration with the v'sori).

Iron Head's crew starts building the battlefield, setting up cameras, and dropping flyers all over town hyping the big event—the bloody debut of *ARENA!*

Creating the battlefield takes several weeks, which should help you push this epic confrontation toward the end of your campaign, preferably after most of the villains have reached Veteran Rank or higher.

Unless the villains have told Big Sis why they've been harassing her gang, she remains oblivious and stays out of the group's way until the match. She figures they either want to run her crew or are simply psychopathic—which may actually be the case, of course.

In any event, Big Sis arrives ready to fight at the appointed time. Move on to the Savage Tale, **Arena!** (page 55).

DEALS WITH DEVILS

Item: The Red Hand's specially marked map of the New York City underground.

Approaching the Red Hand is one of the easier tasks on Dr. Destruction's list. At least at first. Everyone knows where the gangsters have set up shop, so it's just a simple trip to their "emporium" in what used to be the Chelsea Piers waterfront mall. Getting in to see Iron Head Tony himself is a little tougher.

The villains need a good reason (or story)and a Persuasion roll at −2. Unless the group has taken great pains not to be known, assume Tony's bodyguards know them and their powers and take whatever precautions make the most sense. That might include additional bodyguards (use Red Hand Thug, see page 90), enforcers , or even asking certain visitors to wait out in the compound while only one of their group goes up to speak to "da boss."

Eventually, of course, the group should be able to get to Tony and tell whatever story they want. Tony knows what the map is for, so any lies won't go unnoticed. He still makes the deal though—the map is worthless to him, and he has a copy anyway.

"You want the underground map, huh? Yeah. I know the one you're talking about. Ghost made it. Supposed to lead through some secret tunnel down past the sewers and out to the ocean. Piece o' junk if you ask me. The tunnel's there but it's got teeth, capice? An' fins. Mutant k'tharens cast off from the aliens. The place is lousy with 'em, it's flooded, and there's no proof that it goes anywhere anyway. Totally useless.

"But you want it, bring me half a million in goods. Good stuff. No garbage. Food, ammo, drinks, valuables…at our standard rates, of course. Do that and the map's yours. Capice?"

Everyone knows the Ghost. She (or he…no one knows for sure) had no known powers but was a very capable spy who worked primarily for others, gathering intel, secrets, and any other information valuable enough to sell. A Common Knowledge roll recalls that she was in the cordon in the early days, but none of the group has heard anything about her since. Not surprising, given her MO, but *perhaps* a sign too that she found a way out.

Here endeth the negotiations. Iron Head Tony won't accept any other terms (unless the group comes up with something *really* special). He's living like a king here in the post-cordon city and all he wants is more goods to keep things going a few more years while he works out his bigger plan (see page 44).

When the group eventually complies, Iron Head gives them the map and a pair of UV goggles with one hour of battery life remaining. "You'll need these once you're in," he says, without explaining further. "I'd make sure you take good care of 'em."

A SHOW OF FORCE

The villains witness a strange event as they exit Iron Head's compound. A pack of k'tharen mutates rush the front entrance. It's a mad and violent rush that ends in a pool of the shark-men's blood. Read the following aloud, but allow the player characters to jump into the fight if they want.

As you exit the mall you hear heavy gunfire from the front gates. You venture closer to see the carnage and aren't disappointed. A rabid gang of k'tharens run straight up the street, screaming in their strange tongue and clearly out for blood.

You've heard of these horrors before—they're some sort of deranged cast-offs from the alien invaders, dumped into the prison along with the rest of you. They're as big as the aliens' regular shock troops but clearly deranged. Likely no good in an organized force, but an entertaining source of mayhem in this hell hole.

If the villains don't intervene, Iron Head Tony's guards gun the sharks down—but a couple make it to the heavy blasters and almost take one out. If the characters jump out and fight, there are three left in good enough shape to battle. Assuming the villains win, one of Iron Head Tony's lieutenants, a tough, one-eyed woman named Danica Widmark (use the Enforcer stats on page 89, and add the One Eye Hindrance), nods at them and motions at someone inside. A few moments later, one of Tony's gangsters comes out with a box of military rations (four man days of food).

- **K'tharen Mutates (11):** See page 86.

ARENA!

Run this event only near the end of this Plot Point Campaign.

The villains have become such a thorn in the Sykos' side that the elusive Big Sis is finally forced to fight them. She and a number of her captains equal to the player characters agree to fight their rivals at Iron Head Tony's new gladiatorial match, creatively called *ARENA!*

The battle takes place on the top of an eight story building at 524 W 23rd St near his operation at Chelsea Piers. Iron Head's techies have rigged the entire place up with high-definition cameras to capture the action from every angle. Projectors and viewscreens are set up at the Hudson River Greenway (Pier 62 and Pier 63). They're powered by generators and staffed by Red Hand wannabes selling every kind of food they can manage—questionable hot dogs, meats on sticks, cotton candy, and even pizza. Just the smell of these familiar foods drives most New Yorkers crazy, and they're bringing in a *fortune* in valuables for just a taste.

Iron Head has declared the park—and indeed the whole island, though of course he can't enforce it—a safe zone for the day, a 24-hour truce so that everyone can watch the debut of his gladiator game show, *ARENA!*

- **Big Sis and Co (11):** See page 91 for Big Sis' stats and give her a team equal to the player characters. Iron Head Tony and Big Sis are smart, so choose foes who have some chance against the player characters.

THE DOME

Iron Head Tony seems to have a knack for this sort of thing—he designed the battleground himself—a spinning disc dotted with randomly erupting spikes.

Tony's "eggheads" at first scoffed at the idea of being straight out of the old *Flash Gordon* movie, then quickly rethought their reaction when they saw the scowl on the boss' face.

The result is both an engineering marvel and a guarantee of vomit and bloodshed.

The battleground is a 20-foot tall dome of welded rebar, just high enough to allow flying villains to take advantage of their power but not so high they can't escape a determined foe willing to climb a little.

The floor of the dome is 40 feet in diameter and spins like a massive turntable. An iron pole sticking up out of the center holds a bladed arm that can be raised or lowered via pulleys just above the dome at the whim of Iron Tony's controllers.

The whole thing sits atop an eight-story building in the middle of a long New York street that was otherwise rubbled in the fight with the v'sori.

THE DISC

In play, anytime a character's Action Card is a Club, he must make an Agility roll at −2. Failure means a barbed spike erupts up out

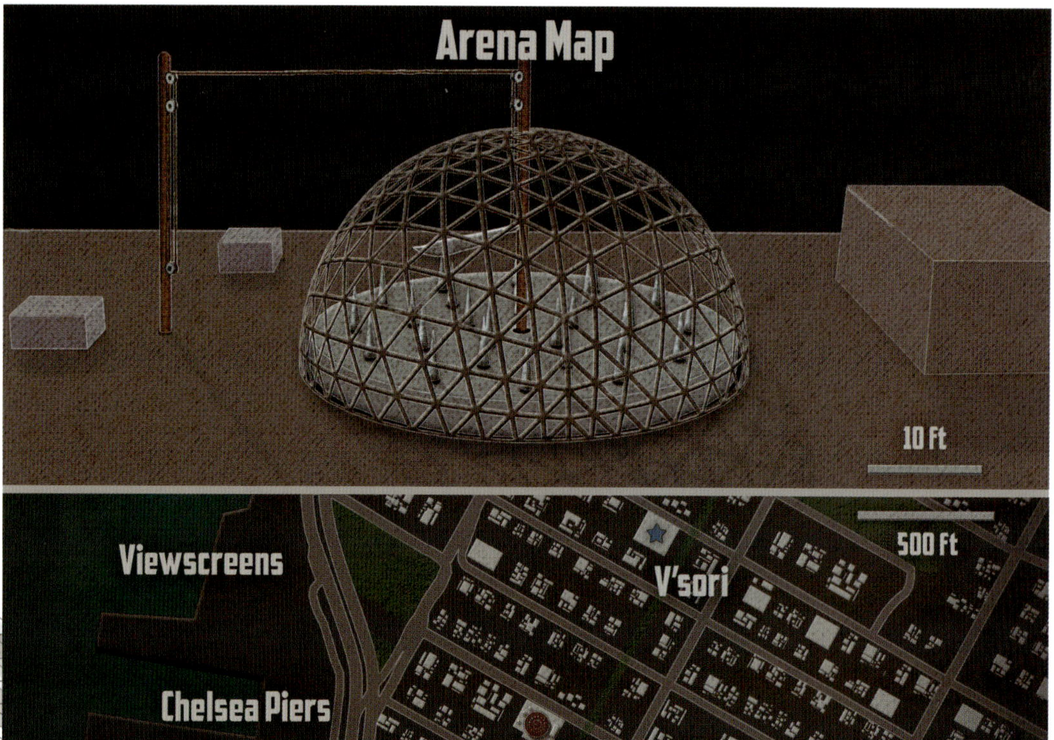

of the disc causing 3d6 damage at AP 4. A critical failure causes 5d6 damage at AP 4.

VIPS

Sure enough, v'sori Warlord Sh'tarka attends the show. K'lent brings her in his mbuna complete with his usual escort. They land on a building a few blocks away and watch through vision enhancers.

Iron Head sends a detachment of his best guards (about a dozen of them) to guard the base of the building as well. He wants a deal with the v'sori and doesn't want any angry prisoner jeopardizing it.

THE CHARM NECKLACE

Getting the charm necklace means taking out Big Sis. Even if they snag it off her during the fight she notices and comes after it with all her ability.

So why all this trouble over a charm necklace? That mystery is resolved in **Escape From New York**, page 57 but the villains can ponder its meaning in the meantime. The thin but strong metal chain holds:

- The ragged remains of three ears.
- A metal ankh symbol taken from the neck of the super heroine named Ankh.
- A finger bone taken from her arch-nemesis, the Owl. He died ignominiously after a bout with Phobos (see Nevermore page 87).
- The remains of a small flash drive. A hole has been drilled through it for the chain.

ESCAPE FROM NEW YORK

Once the villains have all the items they were tasked with gathering, they can contact Firefly. Unless they've arranged something else, he only turns his commlink on at noon each day as promised. Once contacted, he reveals the following:

"Y'know that map you got from the Red Hand? Go to the subway station marked Start and head on in. It's a long, one-way trip, so make sure you have all that stuff Dr. Destruction told you to get or you ain't gonna make it. I don't know where or how you're supposed to use it, but here's the next holoslug. Maybe that will help.

"I've decided to stick around here and see what happens, so you're on your own. No way am I going down into the sewers with those…things. Good luck…or whatever."

Of course Firefly can be "coerced" into joining the group, but only under threat of violence.

When the villains play the next slug, Dr. Destruction appears once again.

"Congratulations, villains. I had every faith you would succeed. Be warned though, that if you didn't follow my instructions to the letter, this plan will not work. You must have the 100 gallons of liquid fear formula, Big Sis' necklace, the deep dive suits, UV goggles, and Iron Head Tony's subway map. If you have all these items, go to the 81st Street Subway Station. The map begins there. Once inside, use the UV goggles to find your way.

"Remember that the Vermintide rules the Red Depths. The fear formula is not for them, so you'll need some other way to battle the swarms. Recruit some help or gather weapons capable of defeating the swarms.

"Use Dr. Phobos' formula just before you don the suits—you'll know when. The formula will not only protect you from the mutants, but will guide you to your exit as well.

"If you survive, I'll see you soon."

With that the holoslug stops and deletes itself. This time, a puff of smoke comes from the holoplayer as well—it's fried.

The villains have been warned. They must be capable of dealing with the Vermintide if they venture beneath the streets. They might be capable of this on their own or they might want to recruit help from among the various gangs. A flamethrower or two (or forcing Firefly to come along) is also highly recommended!

THE SEWERS

The villains now have everything they need to make their escape and hopefully enough power to fight off the Vermintide—which they know waits somewhere beneath the streets.

Their first step to freedom is into the subway system. The trek starts at the 81st Street Subway Station near the Museum of Natural History. Once inside, they can follow the

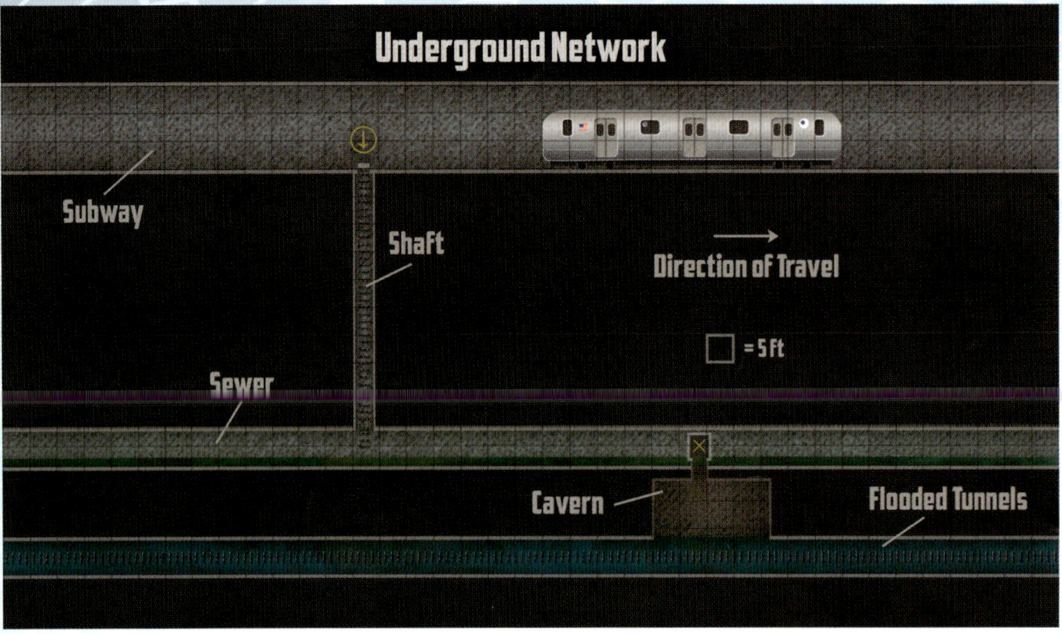

map south. The trek from here is over a mile long, winding through collapsed or blocked sections with no other clear access. It's pitch black, so the villains also need some type of illumination. Hopefully they prepared for this ahead of time.

Along the way the group sees abandoned subway cars and some signs that people once hid down here. Their bedding, empty water bottles, and old food wrappers lie jumbled about in heaps. All of it has been shredded—obviously by rats. A Notice roll or Tracking at +2 also detects thousands (if not tens of thousands) of tiny foot prints over any surface that leaves them.

After a few hundred yards, the villains begin to see one rat, then two, then small packs. The creatures eye the intruders quietly for a while, then begin to chitter as they move along. Play up the tension as the villains move through and over wrecked subway cars, large piles of shifting rubble, and mounds of human and animal bones. The characters can kill or chase off as many rats as they like—there are always more.

This would be an excellent time for an **Interlude** (see *Savage Worlds*).

DOWN THE HATCH

Eventually, the team comes to an access hatch that leads into the sewers. Drawn in invisible paint and visible only with UV goggles or a UV lamp is a circle drawn in invisible paint with a large arrow pointing down directly at it. This is the first mark Ghost left for her companions.

The hatch opens into a dark shaft going straight down into blackness and clearly only wide enough for one character at a time. Make the group decide who's going first!

The bottom of the shaft is 40 feet down and opens into a knee-deep collecting chamber. It smells of filth and rot and obviously hasn't been purged since the fall of New York.

The rats watch as the villains negotiate the pipe. As soon as the party is split in half, the Vermintide attacks from both above and below. Read the following as this terrible ambush occurs:

> *The rats stare at you with baleful black eyes, baring their sharp yellow teeth in hate. It is far more than bestial…it is alien. Those above hear a great rumbling from thousands—perhaps tens of thousands—of chittering rodents approaching in a massive wave.*
>
> *Those below hear a different sound—like that of ocean waves but thicker and slower. A titanic swarm of rats are rushing through the muck.*

The fight starts as a tidal wave of chittering brown hate slams into the villains above and below. The Vermintide has sensed its prey and rushes to consume their tasty flesh. Hopefully the team has prepared to fight this inevitable denizen of the deep places.

The Vermintide attacks with everything it's got. Hit the team with a Vermintide swarm per villain (see page 92). At the start of the fifth round, another swarm per villain plus the core arrives. Only if all swarms are destroyed at once does the core retreat.

If the villains can't defeat the Vermintide, their other option is to run. If they flee back down the tunnels to daylight, each character suffers 2d6 bites each (using the swarm's standard damage) before they make it out. If they rush down into the sewer, the rats suddenly stop about 100 yards away from the hatch—each character suffers only 1d4 bite attacks.

THE FLOODED TUNNELS

Once the Vermintide has been dealt with (or evaded), the villains push on, following the map through the sewers until they come to the section marked with a large glowing X in invisible paint (visible with the UV goggles or lamp).

On the wall below the X is a hexagonal hole—obviously a keyhole of some kind. The key, of course, is the broken pin found on Big Sis' necklace. Once inserted into the hole, something clicks and a concealed door pops open. Beyond it is a slide leading down into darkness.

Move on to **A Great Gnashing of Teeth**.

A GREAT GNASHING OF TEETH

Beyond the four-foot diameter portal is a short slide that drops into a cavern filled with the distinctive smell of sea water!

A Common Knowledge roll at −4 or Knowledge (History) at −2 recalls a Nazi villain called Thule ran a spy ring in New York during World War II. It was speculated at the time that he and his agents were getting in and out of the city via U-boats and underwater tunnels, but none were ever found—at least that the public knew about. If this is one of them, the tunnel is deeper than anyone thought (deep enough to go out under the v'sori cordon, in fact!).

Sh'tarka and her pet scientist M'oro are using the old base to create her new k'tharen super soldiers—"tharn," in the shark men's own language. It is synonymous with both "the perfect warrior" and the living avatars of their red-toothed god, Mog.

The lower tunnels are full of M'oro's failed experiments—the cast-off mutates. The upper chambers are where the scientist and tharn, now perfected, await Sh'tarka. A handful of tharn serve as armed guards for M'oro in case of trouble. While they are always wary of human interlopers, their main concern is the increasingly agitated population of mutates. The creatures have begun to resent their cruel masters and signs of rebellion are imminent.

The rest of the tharn, a half-pod of 48, are in stasis tubes ready for transport and Sh'tarka's attack on the Overmind. They rest in cargo containers in the sub pens awaiting pickup (see The Sub Pen, page 63).

1) ENTRANCE

It's time to put on the dive suits for those who require oxygen. Dive lamps are also highly recommended.

This is also the time to pour the fear formula into the water. The passages the team must travel down are filled with dozens of ravenous k'tharen mutates. The villains' special deep diving suits protect them from the serum while sending most of the deranged shark-men swimming far away from its taint for hours. As importantly, thick, viscous globs of the stuff follow the natural flow of the cavern to the ocean—showing the escapees which way to go.

If the group forgets this detail, remind them, then read the following:

> *You follow the green globs as they drift toward what you can only assume is the ocean. It's an easy swim, the current pulls you along through tight tunnels that slowly give way to larger caverns…all submerged hundreds of feet beneath New York City.*
>
> *Strangely, there are handholds along the side of the tunnel—stainless steel since they show no signs of rust. A person could use this to push themselves against the current toward the hatch you entered from if desired.*

Soon you begin to see junctions in the tunnel, but the current pulls you—and the fear formula—down the center.

The cross channels lead to the warrens of the pitiful k'tharen mutate cast-offs. The formula has terrified the creatures so they hide in concentrated mobs in their deepest holes. If the villains venture down into these lairs, they find numerous mutates in a state of frenzied panic. There's little else in their caves except bones and spare bits of metal or other "treasures" they've salvaged from their sad prison. This is a *very* dangerous proposition and should be avoided.

2) THE SPAWNING CHAMBER

Just before the group reaches the next room, a large dark shape rushes from the southern tunnel. It bumps into the lead villain then jets frantically into the chamber ahead. The unseen thing continues on its way in a swirl of debris and detritus without causing any real harm, but it should unnerve the lead character greatly.

The character doesn't get a good look at it even if she can see in the dark—the turbid water, cramped tunnel, and frantic nature of the "attack" just happen too fast. In fact, it's a single k'tharen mutate driven mad by the fear formula, but this one has returned to where it was birthed rather than flee into the natural chasms like the rest. Use this encounter purely for effect.

Read the following when the group enters the next chamber.

You move cautiously into a large, seemingly round chamber filled with thick, waist-high sea grass. Leathery pods the length and width of your arm stream from their tops. Artificial globes of some sort are scattered around the room, giving it an eerie red glow. They emanate warmth.

In the center of the room is a wretched k'tharen. The alien flails around miserably, holding his head and gargling a scream. He has clearly been affected by Phobos' fear formula. His spastic seizure knocks dozens of pods free. One of them swirls about the cavern, momentarily backlit by light of the globes. Within the pod you see a squirming, fish-like thing with jagged teeth—k'tharen spawn!

The k'tharen mutate struggles to remain here and protect the egg-cases. He has promised his life to the pod and will die before he breaks that vow.

K'Tharen Chambers

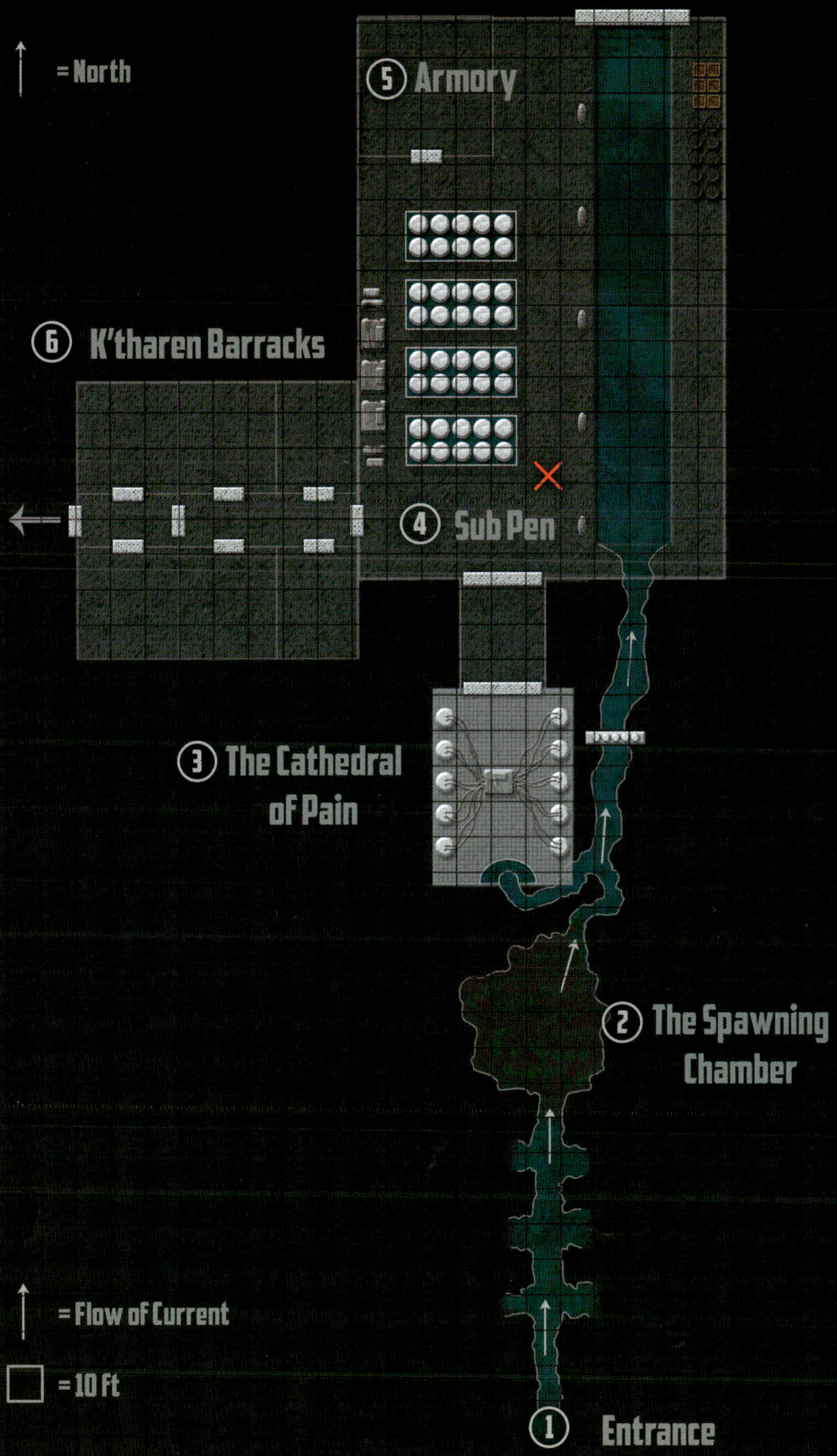

Let the team do what they want to the embattled fin. He's dangerous if they get up close, but if left alone continues to spasm uncontrollably, fighting phantasms in his tortured mind. Should they get close enough to see his face, the villains get one more surprise—he has a large, single red eye.

- **K'tharen Mutate:** The creature is treated as actively Berserk (per the Edge) while affected by the fear formula. See page 86.

3) THE CATHEDRAL OF PAIN

The villains can press on once they've decided what to do about the mutated fin.

In the back of the spawning chamber is another tunnel. You can feel the gentle current pulling you on. Shortly after, it branches. One branch leads upward and you can see pale blue light somewhere ahead. The current continues on to the east, but a barred gate blocks access.

The green globules of fear formula are gone now. You cross your fingers and hope they have already caused most of the mutated fins to flee. Battling scores of these creatures in their natural element does not seem wise.

The tunnel where the current leads is blocked by reinforced titanium bars. The party shouldn't be able to get through, but if they're truly persistent, hit them with a few mutates who have regained their senses. If they *still* persist, let them cut through the bars and move the encounter in this room to the sub pen. It's more dramatic and natural if they go up through the Cathedral of Pain, but it won't ruin the adventure if they pass by that room. Just make sure they get the information somehow.

More likely, the group moves up the passage and exits the lighted pool into the Cathedral of Pain, as M'oro calls it. This is where the spawn are trained to hate. They hate humans, they hate "regular" k'tharen, and most of all they hate the Overmind!

You swim up a tight tunnel toward the blue light and emerge into a pool at the far end of a rectangle room. The tunnels thus far seemed carved from the bedrock, but this is a regular room with tile walls and floors.

You climb out of the pool and see five pods on either wall, all connected to a glowing control panel at the center of the room—complete with v'sori letters. At the far end of the room is a massive 20-foot wide blast door—adorned with an old and fading swastika.

The room was once a staging area for Thule's German assault platoon. The plan was to use the handholds along the underwater tunnels to pull themselves against the current to the subway system. From there they would emerge beneath New York City and wreak whatever havoc their master designed.

M'oro has used the room for an even darker purpose. Along the walls are upright pods designed to hold a single mutate each. At the top of the pod are two wires ending in some kind of prickly pad. These go directly onto the subject's head and interface with the k'tharen's brain.

If a player character touches the pad, he gets a brief vision of the screaming Overmind! The sensation is far too intense for the character to maintain, but he instantly understands the machine's purpose—it's to make these subjects *hate* the v'sori master! This is the first real clue of Sh'tarka's betrayal.

In the center of the room is a v'sori control panel attached to the machines via numerous heavy cables. The screens are in v'sori and very complex, even for a native speaker, but a few minutes of investigation determines the panel feeds images to the pods…and also something else. While the exact principle is beyond the current understanding of the villains, she slowly deduces the machine feeds raw emotion into the recipient's brain. Strong images combined with intense emotions condition the subject to hate whatever is shown—which of course is exactly what's happening here.

KNOCK, KNOCK!

After the villains have had a few moments to uncover the clues, the large blast door at the north end of the room slides up to reveal a dozen k'tharen. These fins look different, however. They're bigger and their skin shines gloss black. These are the tharn come to protect their master!

Somewhere beyond the tharn the villains hear a more ominous sound—the heavy clunk of enormous metal feet. The tharn attack in the first round. On the next, a massive Nazi war machine stomps into the cathedral! Written across the front of the war machine are the words DIE BIESTE, or "The Beast" in German. It's an *incredibly* tough threat for our Street Level villains so feel free to warn them. This threat may require every bit of tactical knowledge and planning they can manage.

- **Tharn (12):** The fins are armed with pulse rifles. See page 87.
- **The Beast:** M'oro found this leftover war machine in the base and has given it a few upgrades in his spare time.

THE BEAST

The Beast was created by the Nazis to defend the secret base. It has an MG34 machine-gun on a shoulder mount, a giant pincer for one arm, and a massive buzzsaw on the other. It has a crude but effective AI, slightly augmented by M'oro so it won't attack him or the k'tharen.

Note that the Beast has Heavy Armor, meaning some of the player characters might not be able to hurt it *at all*. This is intentional—it's supposed to be *extremely* tough and encourage them to use teamwork, tactics, or clever tricks to defeat.

Attributes: Agility d4, Smarts d4, Spirit d8, Strength d12+8, Vigor d10

Skills: Fighting d8, Notice d6, Shooting d6

Pace: 4; **Parry:** 6; **Toughness:** 18 (6)

Gear: MG34 on shoulder mount (Range 30/60/120, RoF 3, Damage 2d8+1, no recoil penalty for mount).

- **Armor +6:** Heavy.
- **Buzzsaw Hand:** Str+2d6, AP 4, Reach 1.
- **Improved Frenzy:** The Beast can attack with both its hands (and its machine gun) in one round at no penalty.
- **Pincer Hand:** Str+2d6, Reach 1. Can be used to grapple.
- **Sweep:** The Beast can attack all opponents up to a Reach of 1 with one of its hands each round per the Improved Sweep Edge. It can't Sweep with *both* hands each round, but it can Sweep with one and attack with the other normally.
- **Toughness:** Toughness +5. Hardy.

4) THE SUB PEN

While the party fights the Beast and tharn, M'oro prepares his next line of defense. Two more tharn crouch beside him from behind a makeshift barrier of old machine parts at the spot marked X.

Beyond the chamber you're in is another, much larger room. In the center are several large containers the size of rail cars. They're clear—like fish tanks—and hold dozens of the black-skinned k'tharen in clear stasis tubes.

Right of the containers is a long pool leading to another large blast door—it's an old Nazi sub pen!

Running along the left hand wall are old computers and control panels.

Just in front of the containers are two more of the black-skinned k'tharen behind a metal barricade of old machines. They glare at you menacingly, ready for action.

Another figure, a v'sori, squats behind them. He's furiously banging on what looks like a remote control and hisses as the heavy blast doors between you and the aliens sputter and grind. He's trying to close them but they're stuck! It's time to act!

The blast doors between areas 3 and 4 have indeed malfunctioned, giving the villains a chance to get into the sub pen. If they wait another round, the doors slowly start to close, so they should push forward

immediately. Once the doors are shut, they can be opened with the correct code (only M'oro knows it), and are an immense Toughness 16.

Another reason to press forward quickly becomes apparent as well. The mutates hiding in the rest of the complex have started to emerge from the pool in the Cathedral of Pain.

Suddenly you hear splashing, snarling, and growling from behind you. You glance back and see hideously mutated k'tharen rising from the pool you used to enter the pod room! They seem to be gathering in force, waiting until their numbers are great enough to attack!

To your front, the v'sori with the remote looks in shock and surprise at the water in the sub pen—it's rippling! A sub is coming!

5) ARMORY

The fins keep two dozen pulse rifles, 200 fusion grenades, and spare sets of combat armor here.

6) BARRACKS

The fins and M'oro live and sleep here.

REINFORCEMENTS...FROM ABOVE!

The two remaining tharn do their best to hold off the villains but are doomed. More worrying is what's happening behind the villains—the mutates begin to attack and there are *dozens* of the tragic and bloodthirsty things.

At the start of the next round, the large door at the far end of the sub pen opens and a v'sori barracuda sails into the bay! It immediately opens fire on anyone in clear sight but takes great care not to hit the precious containers.

The following round, Sh'tarka herself, K'lent, and their personal escorts emerge from the barracuda and join the fray. Sh'tarka would love to just pull the barracuda back out and leave the villains to their fate, but she can't—her tharn are ready and she knows the humans are likely to destroy the sleeping warriors if she leaves them unprotected.

ENEMIES AHEAD, FOES BEHIND!

The villains have a mob of angry mutates at their back and Sh'tarka and her forces ahead, supported by the deck gun of the barracuda. It's a tough fight, but it's certainly not impossible. The group does have a couple of other options, however.

First, the mutates might be convinced or lured into fighting Sh'tarka and her cohorts. Their fear of M'oro and his tharn have kept them repressed so far, but perhaps sensing the change in situation—or maybe regaining courage after Phobos' fear formula, they're ready to revolt. If successful, the group can then take the barracuda out through the cordon.

The villains might also threaten to destroy the hibernating tharn somehow. If they seem capable of doing so, Sh'tarka is willing to make some kind of deal:

"Wait! We have the same goal. These sacred warriors are the tharn. They are the embodiment of what the k'tharen believe are perfect warriors—even avatars of their god. M'oro and I plan to use them to overthrow the Overmind—the creature that ordered us to attack your planet!

"Invading Earth was a foolish and petty move, and many of my kind resent it. I can escort you beyond the cordon and give you your freedom. Leave us be and we will kill *the Overmind for you. That should give your 'Omega Resistance' an opportunity to win your planet's freedom.*

"Do we have an accord?"

Sh'tarka is true to her word—if she has to be. If she gets a *clear* chance to double-cross the foolish monkeys, however, and it's nearly certain she can get away with it, she's more than happy to do so.

Otherwise, Sh'tarka ferries the group onto the barracuda and out the channel. The cordon parts for her and she emerges a few miles off shore in the Atlantic. There she gives the humans a skiff and bids them farewell.

Where the only beings ever to escape from the New York City Prison go after that is up to them...

FIN FINALE?

This is likely the end of this *Necessary Evil* campaign, but a future book explores the cosmic level heroes and villains of the setting—and reveals the fate of Sh'tarka's desperate plan.

SAVAGE TALES

On the following pages are more adventures you can use in your own campaign or between episodes of *Breakout!*

All of these are tied to location descriptions or events during the Plot Point Campaign, as noted by this symbol: ✦

Wild Card characters are noted with the symbol of Dr. Destruction:

BRING ME THE HEAD OF NEVERMORE!

Before the invasion, a thug named Carlos Ragsdale was in the right place at the right time. The legendary hero Owl suffered a particularly bad reaction to Phobos' fear formula and staggered into an alley where Carlos and his fellow gang members were mugging some poor sap. Carlos sensed something wasn't right and decided to fight. In a blur of action even he doesn't remember, his knife flashed and the Owl lay dead at his feet.

Carlos Ragsdale became an instant legend He had killed one of the city's most famous defenders.

Soon after, the thug was offered a job with the Red Hand. Carlos performed well enough, but managed to survive and keep his position after the cordon. Since then, he's had two close calls with the Owl's former sidekick, Nevermore (once the Raven).

Carlos knows Nevermore is a killer now and is terrified of running into the vengeful protege. He never leaves the protection of the Red Hand mall under any circumstances, and thus far has stayed out of the deadly Nevermore's clutches. But everyone knows Nevermore is watching Carlos, and it's only a matter of time before he avenges the Owl's miserable end.

This story starts in one of two ways. If you're running the Breakout! Plot Point Campaign, Phobos has asked the villains to retrieve plutonium from the Ice Queen's gun. Nevermore already slew the Ice Queen, however, and carries her lethal weapon on his belt (see The Ice Queen on page 72 for the full story). The villains should realize that the best bait for drawing out Nevermore is Carlos Ragsdale himself. If this is the situation, proceed to **Bait and Switch**.

If you're not running the Plot Point Campaign, Carlos Ragsdale is under a lot of pressure from Iron Head Tony and the rest of the Red Hand to step up his gang. He lucked into his position from the start and isn't quite as swift as his peers. Carlos believes if he can get rid of Nevermore, he can make some moves, step up his game, and get the respect he deserves. He might even stop having all those nightmares. In this case, Ragsdale quietly hires the villains to help. He doesn't offer himself as bait.

BAIT AND SWITCH

The villains can come up with any plan they want to lure Nevermore out into the open so they can defeat or capture him, but there are a few caveats.

First, Ragsdale won't offer himself up as bait. He's far too paranoid. He won't even leave the compound. He's six feet of nervous energy who hasn't slept well since he killed the Owl and has had to act tougher and more competent than he really is.

Also, Nevermore has several spies in the Red Hand and knows most of its business. He doesn't have access to the inner circle or Iron Head Tony's more secretive actions, but he has fairly detailed information about everything at Ragsdale's level. He could *have* Carlos killed if he wants, but Nevermore wants that honor for himself.

A few other obvious ploys present themselves. A character with the ability to disguise himself (naturally or via a power like mimic) could pose as Carlos and let himself be seen leaving the compound. It might take several occurrences to establish a pattern Nevermore might pick up on, but eventually the vigilante should learn about it.

Another plan might be to simply kidnap Ragsdale and put out word that the villains are willing to trade him for the Ice Queen's gun. This is a particularly bad move, unfortunately. Nevermore will be prepared for a trap (see below), but more importantly, the Red Hand can't let this stand—it makes them look weak. Iron Head won't agree to it if the villains ask him to look the other way or let it slide until Nevermore is killed, either—it just makes the Red Hand look too weak. Especially if it doesn't work.

Let the party come up with any plan they want. The more planning they do together, the better. They are super villains after all, and this is the kind of scheming they do.

Nevermore should have a good chance of seeing through all but the most cunning plans. He's incredibly canny from his years training with the Owl, and he's riddled the Red Hand's compound with spies and listening devices.

If the group comes up with a truly foolproof plan, let them carry it out and allow the cards to fall where they may. Otherwise, Nevermore sets a countertrap if he thinks the bad guys are out to get him.

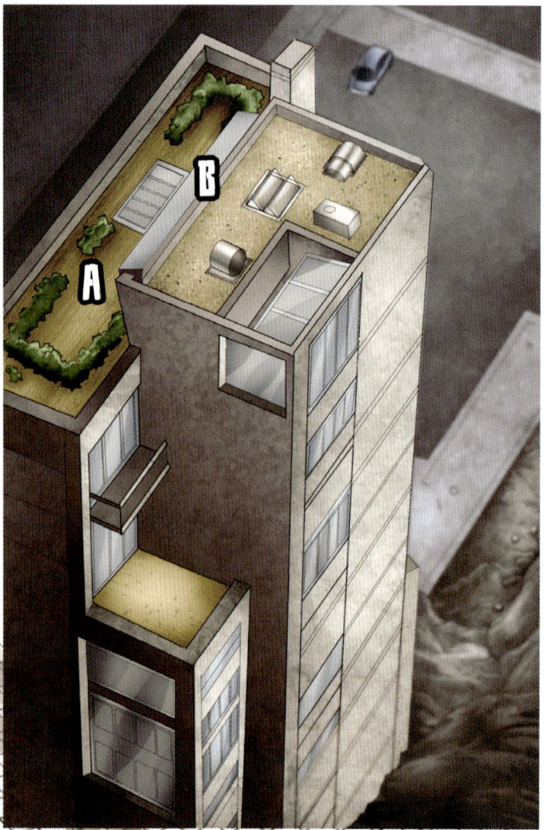

IT'S A TRAP!

Nevermore uses his various informants and spies (most of whom don't even know they're working for him) to put out the word he can be found in a former private storage building across from Chelsea Piers, at 793 11th Avenue.

Depending on the situation, the rumor either says he's established a lair in the building, is waiting to battle "Ragsdale's minions" to end it once and for all, or is willing to pay for Ragsdale himself. The Game Master should tailor the message and setup to fit the villains' actions. Either way, it's a trap.

The top of the 20-story building is a rectangle with skylights into the offices below and shrubbery along the edges. The roof door lets out onto the garden terrace at Area A. Nevermore waits at the spot marked B. When the villains emerge from the doorway (or climb or fly to the rooftop) read the following.

You emerge on the rooftop to see a figure backlit dramatically by the (moon/sun). Though you can see no details due to the lighting, there's little doubt this is the hero known as Nevermore.

"That's far enough. This device in my hand is a dead man's switch. There's enough C4 under your feet to blow the roof out onto 11th Avenue. Maybe even over to that playground across the street. Where I'm standing is perfectly safe, but where

you are...well...that's death. No death trap, no prattling monologue to give you time to escape. Just death. Fast and brutal.

"Now let's talk about why you're here."

The Worst Kind of Negotiations

What happens next depends on why they're here and what Nevermore has learned about them. If the group has Ragsdale (or a lookalike and Nevermore hasn't discovered their plans already), he'll actually make the trade—his mentor's murderer for the Ice Queen's gun. He then tells the group to leave and Ragsdale is never seen again.

If the villains don't have Ragsdale, Nevermore might make a deal. He might allow all but one of them—someone in the group at least a few of the other miscreants cares about—to leave and go try to get Ragsdale. It's a long shot, especially in a hurry, but Nevermore is generous. He gives them till dusk, dawn, or roughly four hours. If the villains agree, he leaves (so he isn't standing on the rooftop waiting and exposed) but tells them he can see everything they're doing. He monitors the rooftop from hidden button cams stationed around it. If the hostage tries to leave, he blows the roof.

If the villains can somehow disable Nevermore's detonator (such as with a power or shooting it out of his hand), he dives off the back of the building. Wings expand between his arms and his torso and he bolts off the top of the roof to the east, gliding along the lower buildings to the other side of 10th avenue.

If the group has a mind controller, character with a *stun* or *paralysis* power, or someone who can *jinx* or disable the dead man's switch, then the silhouette of Nevermore is a mannequin with a remote speaker in its mouth area dressed in a spare costume—it takes a Notice roll at −4 to spot this at first. After a minute or so goes by, give the group another chance at no penalty. At that point, Nevermore admits it and says he's a safe distance away watching everything.

In short, do everything you can to make Nevermore a smart and dangerous opponent. If the group outsmarts him, however, let them! That is the end goal, after all. But don't make it easy.

Raise the Roof!

If the worst comes and can't be stopped, Nevermore blows the roof. It angles up and west as a shattered rectangular block into 11th Avenue. The blast itself causes no damage to the villains, but everyone who crashes to earth with it suffers 12d6+10 damage (the extra two dice are for the rubble).

Resolution

If Nevermore gets away with the Ice Queen's pistol, the group can attempt to set another trap, keep looking for him, or come up with any other plan they think might work. This could take days or even weeks or months while they go about their other tasks—that's perfectly fine. Nevermore isn't omniscient, but he is clever and he does everything in his power to gather information and fight on his own terms when he can.

If the villains eventually defeat him, they get the Ice Queen's gun and the plutonium nugget inside (see **The Essence of Fear**, page 48). Otherwise, they might be forced to go after Neutron instead—see page 75.

Cloudy with a Chance of Doom

The v'sori patrol the cordon from above the energy field in a mbuna transport staffed with Battle Masters and fins. One of the Battle Masters, K'lent, occasionally drops goods to the "ants" below, then watches them fight over whatever prize he's decided to give them. K'lent most often drops food—he knows how much the prisoners miss steak, pizza, cheeseburgers, and other American staples.

The goods are dropped in special impact-absorbing boxes that allow them to survive the 200+ foot fall. This isn't to say the toppings stay where they were placed on the pizza, but at least they're all in the same box.

The Game Master might "bless" the party with one of K'lent's drops at any time, or it might occur as a result of the **Above Encounter Table**. The drop starts just above the cordon and falls wherever air currents,

K'LENT'S DROP

Roll a d6 to determine what the drop contains.

d6	Prize
1	**Hot Food:** A box full of burgers, hot dogs, pizza, Indian food, or other rare treats for 20 people (value $2,000).
2	**Newspapers:** A collection of print newspapers or magazines. The news seems to talk about how great the v'sori are for humanity, and how bad Dr. Destruction and his Omega "terrorist" cells are for everyone.
3	**Tainted Food:** K'lent has poisoned the food from 1, above, with some undetectable alien virus! Anyone who eats it must make a Vigor roll or suffer severe stomach issues (Exhaustion) for the next 48 hours.
4	**Weapons:** The crate contains a box full of weapons. Roll three times on the Weapons Sub-Table on page 27.
5	**Canned Food:** The crate contains an assortment of canned goods, mostly beans, corn, Spaghetti-Os, or dog/cat food. There are 2d20 cans worth $20 each.
6	**Bomb:** K'lent's cruelty knows no bounds. Concealed beneath a layer of canned goods is a bomb. When the crate is opened it detonates for 4d6 damage in a Large Burst Template.

gravity, and obstacles take it—usually within a four-square-block area or so.

Everyone in the neighborhood makes a run for the goods, so the villains must be fast if they want them for themselves.

Finding and getting to the drop is a Dramatic Task. The villains roll as a group using a cooperative Streetwise test to navigate the streets and heights of the city.

If a Complication comes up, *each* character must make an Agility test at −4 or fall behind and no longer be able to contribute to the group roll. (If the drop is found, these characters show up d4+2 rounds later.)

If the task isn't completed in five actions, the drop is found by others. Roll a d6 to see who: 1–4: 2d6 Gangers; 5–6: 4d6 Scavengers.

GANG WAR!

Run this tale when most of the villains are a few Advances beyond Heroic.

This Savage Tale is larger than most. In fact, it could serve as an entire Plot Point Campaign on its own depending on how you want to run it. The tale revolves around a massive war between all the various gangs and factions, and even the rise of a new and very powerful group. The player characters can't help but get caught up in it and must create their own gang or side with one of the others. If they don't, they face almost certain extinction.

THE COURT WILL RISE

Corben Malone was one of New York City's toughest judges. His nickname in the US District Court was the "Hanging Judge." When the k'tharen attacked, Corben, a former Major in the US Army's Judge Advocate General's Corp (JAGC), dropped his robe in favor of a uniform and volunteered for the defense of the city.

His fights were brutal and efficient. Several articles were written about the "Battlin' Judge of Long Island."

Then disaster struck. An encounter with a group of fins went badly and left the major in a coma at the VA New York Harbor hospital for months. When the second invasion began and the v'sori betrayed the Earth, the hospital was struck by an alien bomb and leveled.

Judge Malone was buried alive. But his own super powers began to kick in. He survived, dormant and trapped in his nightmares of his city burning. Super "heroes" failed the people and super villains exploited them.

When he finally awoke, Corben crawled out from under tons of rubble to find his nightmares had come true. The Big Apple had not only fallen, it had become an alien prison!

The soldier, lawyer, and judge staggered through the streets, still dressed in the shreds of his hospital gown. He watched as the strong preyed on the weak and the city continued to fall into depravity. Then the Sykos attacked. A group of them stabbed him with knives and hit him with iron pipes—but he barely felt it. He tore them to pieces with his bare hands. A group of bystanders, hiding in the shadows nearby, came out and cheered.

Corben knew what the people needed. They needed justice. He was sealed in a prison. Fine. Then he would become the Judge.

The Judge fashioned a new costume for himself and began dispensing justice. Soon after, he was joined by a woman he calls Jury and another man called Executioner.

THE NIGHT COURT

Judge, Jury, and Executioner—collectively the "Night Court"—start what quickly becomes a gang war by cleaning the Sykos out of the Lower East Side. Big Sis retaliates in force, sending squads of her grinning goons into the area to find the three troublemakers and put the hurt on anyone who supports them.

What follows is a sample timeline of events and ways to involve the player characters in the action. The timeline is broken up into a number of events that can be run as you see fit. They should be interspersed with the characters' other activities, such as their scavenger hunt or any personal missions they're pursuing.

GANG WAR EVENTS

The events below occur as you, the Game Master, see fit, but each is generally designed to occur over a period of about 10 days.

EVENT 1: JUDGED!

The Judge begins his campaign of "justice" by attacking the Sykos. His killing spree culminates in the execution of a half-dozen gangers left hanging from the (shattered) video screen in Times Square.

Spraypainted over their heads is a single ominous word: "JUDGED!"

EVENT 2: GOOD FOR BUSINESS

The villains see a long line of buyers outside Iron Head Tony's buying guns or bullets for protection. The already outrageous prices of firearms and ammunition have doubled.

If questioned, the buyers say the mysterious Judge has been joined by two other super villains, Jury and Executioner. Together, they call themselves the "Night Court." No one has ever heard of these villains before.

EVENT 2: THE MOB RULES!

The Night Court begins to attract followers. Outcast gangers and scavs calling themselves the "Lynch Mob" begin taking over territory on the Lower East Side. They call for the heads of the Red Hand, Sykos, Harlem Knights, and anyone who opposes the Night Court.

RUNNING THE GANG WAR

This Savage Tale is designed to involve the player characters in the politics of the New York City Prison. They can forge alliances with the other factions, recruit followers, and make dire nemeses.

Put a little effort into some of the nonplayer characters the villains encounter—especially some of the minions they might rally to their cause, or recurring minions of their rivals. A friendly doctor who hates one of their rivals and can patch the villains up after a nasty fight, or the "street rat" who brings them his last soda after saving his friends (even if that wasn't their intent) makes the game much more personal and memorable.

FORMING A GANG

The villains can form their *own* gang too. Visit our website at **www.peginc.com** for a free add-on for this book that allows your player characters to form their own faction in the New York City Gang War!

RED HAND BOUNTY

After **Event 3: Massacre at Chelsea Piers,** Iron Head Tony gets serious. He kicks out scavs and other "non-combatants" (a mistake as many of them join rival gangs) and takes in as many gangers as possible.

He also makes an offer to the player characters they shouldn't refuse.

Tony offers to knock $50K off the price of his underworld map every time they increase the Red Hand's Reputation, and $25K every time they *decrease* the Rep of the Sykos or Lynch Mob.

Tony doesn't care about "those loser Outliers" (Event 6) or the Harlem Knights unless they gain a Reputation of 8 or higher. Then he offers the same Bounty on them.

If the group already has the map, he pays $10K in credit for either action.

EVENT 3: MASSACRE AT CHELSEA PIERS

Sometime when the villains aren't around, Judge, Jury, and Executioner attack the long line of buyers outside Chelsea Piers. The slaughter is terrible and the Red Hand gets a figurative black eye for failing to protect their patrons.

The characters hear about this secondhand—you don't want them encountering Corben and his followers yet.

Iron Head Tony calls for the Night Court's heads.

EVENT 4: LET THEM EAT CAKE

Iron Head Tony sends a negotiator to the Sykos. He hopes the psychopaths will call a truce long enough to deal with these Lynch Mob nutjobs. But the Sykos do what they do best and send the delegates back in cake boxes. Small ones.

The Red Hand declares open war on the Lynch Mob and the Sykos. He sends a runner for the villains and makes them an offer. See **Red Hand Bounty** for the offer he makes.

Begin tracking each faction's **Reputation** now (see below).

EVENT 5: ALL-OUT WAR

The gang war is in full force. Violence escalates and anyone the villains meet in the street is likely to shoot first and ask questions later. Corpses fill the avenues and begin to attract rats.

The effects of this phase of the Gang War are threefold:

- All gang encounters double in size during the Gang War. If a group of 2d6 Gangers are encountered, for example, and a 7 is rolled, there are 14 instead. All encounters are automatically hostile unless the villains are allied with them.
- The Red Hand stops selling to anyone they don't consider an ally. The villains must resort to scavenging if they need ammo, food, or other goods.
- The smell of blood fuels the growth of the Vermintide. Add two additional swarms anytime it's encountered until the Gang War is over.

EVENT 6: RISE OF THE OUTLIERS

The struggle gives rise to a new gang called the Outliers. They're lead by a super-powered woman named Shrill. She takes in everyone terrorized by the other gangs and quickly becomes a significant player.

Their base is in the Beacon Theatre west of Central Park. They mostly keep to themselves but a few early victories against Sykos and the Lynch Mob give them enough cred to swell to a few dozen gangers and three times that in scavs.

WHAT'S A VILLAIN TO DO?

So what are the villains to do in the middle of this gang war? That's entirely up to them. They can wait it out, choose sides, play factions off against each other, or even form their own gang (**Forming a Gang** on page 69).

REPUTATION

Each gang starts with the "Rep" listed below. At the start of each day, roll a d20 on the **Reputation Table** and add a point to the corresponding gang. Then roll a second d20 and *subtract* a point from the listed faction. If the same faction is rolled, it makes gains during the day and loses it that night. Easy come, easy go.

The player characters can affect Reputation by good old-fashioned thrashing. Each time the villains defeat a group of at least a dozen foes of a particular gang, roll a die. Even, their gang's Reputation increases by 1. Odd, the rival gang's Reputation decreases by 1 instead.

This can only happen once per day, per gang regardless of how many scum they thrash.

REPUTATION

d20	Gang	Starting Rep
1–3	Red Hand	6
4–5	Harlem Knights	4
6–12	Lynch Mob	4
13–15	Outliers	3
16–20	Sykos	6

VICTORY & DEFEAT

If any of the gangs reach a Reputation of 10 they emerge victorious and the Gang War is over. Should any gang bottom out so badly their Rep reaches 0, they're defeated. Both instances are covered below.

See the Running a Gang sidebar for what happens if the player characters form a gang that reaches 0 or 10 Reputation.

THE RED HAND

A victorious Red Hand eventually gets back to business as usual. For at least 2d6 days, however, they close up shop and regroup. The villains must find their cheese puffs and Bubbly Fizz soda elsewhere.

The Red Hand's defeat is a disaster for everyone. Chaos ensues, there's no central place to find necessary supplies, and the lesser gangs rise unchecked. The three most powerful gangs at the end of the war battle on through the end of the campaign with no clear victor.

If this happens, Iron Head Tony (or a visionary replacement) decides to put all his effort into *ARENA!* instead. This allows the Savage Tale of the same name to continue as needed (page 55).

HARLEM KNIGHTS

Victory for the Knights, however improbable, means a truce with whoever is left of the Night Court. Law and order begin to take hold and the three gangs at the bottom are scattered. The Knights expand their territory, secure more equipment, and start reinforcing the most basic laws—something that is very likely to rankle the player characters' feathers. Judge, Jury, Executioner, and Full Auto become the Harlem Knights' uneasy allies.

If the Knights are defeated, the Sykos' power grows. Their ranks swell with the outcasts and survivors of other gangs. Add +1d10 additional Sykos any time they're encountered for the rest of the campaign. Wild Card leaders should get an extra Edge or die type in Fighting or Shooting to reflect their battle experience as well.

LYNCH MOB

If the Lynch Mob is victorious, the two gangs with the lowest scores are defeated. The Night Court rules with a chaotic and bloodthirsty hand. Anyone who isn't with them is against them. Anytime another gang (that still exists) is encountered, roll a die. If the result is odd, replace it with a Lynch Mob instead, and add +1d10 to their numbers.

If the Lynch Mob reaches a Reputation of 0, they're not defeated—they're just scattered and demoralized. To actually put an end to this uprising requires defeating Judge, Jury, and Executioner. At this point, the Night Court decides the player characters are responsible for defeating "the people's will." They target the villains, perhaps setting a trap or challenging them to a public fight.

It doesn't matter if the villains have steered clear of the Night Court—for whatever reason, Judge Malone decides *they* are the real cause of the city's ills.

If Malone proves victorious in this final fight, the Lynch Mob snatches victory from defeat. Assuming the Night Court (or at least Judge) is beaten, however, the mob disperses and things return to normal.

OUTLIERS

Victory for Shrill's gang is (soon after) the same as defeat. The day after her "victory," the Night Court tracks her down and slaughters her. The Gang War continues but the Outliers are no longer part of it. Ignore any Reputation rolls that point to them (don't reroll—just ignore it).

SYKOS

Victory for the Sykos is bad for everyone. Their ranks swell with scavs looking to join the winning side and Big Sis puts them right to work. She destroys the two lowest remaining gangs then assaults and takes over the Red Hand's Chelsea Piers warehouse. Iron Head Tony (or one of his lieutenants) survives as a new minion and focuses his attention on *ARENA!* instead (see the **Arena!** Savage Tale on page 55).

Add +1d10 additional Sykos to any encounter group if they win the Gang War. Wild Card leaders get an extra two combat Edges or skills to reflect their hard-earned battle experience.

If the Sykos are defeated, Big Sis goes into hiding for a while. If she "dies," she returns one way or another, at least until she fulfills her role on *ARENA!* Maybe the Big Sis who was defeated was a double, or she simply gained a new power after her death such as *regeneration*.

In this case, the Sykos scatter but survive as independent bands for the duration of this adventure. Reduce their numbers by d3 any time they're encountered, and they cannot summon reinforcements regardless of where they're found.

THE ICE QUEEN

Soon after the cordon was erected, a villainess known as the Ice Queen set out to take over one of the neighborhoods. She was pretty, popular, and had a powerful ice gun she used to freeze—and kill—anyone who opposed her. One dark and rainy night, Nevermore came after her. The two fought an epic battle on the rooftops of midtown before the Ice Queen finally slipped off the rooftop—on a patch of ice created by her own gun.

Rumors spread that Nevermore threw the Ice Queen off the 12th story rooftop. He did nothing to correct them. But he did collect her gun and has used it on several occasions since. Most everyone already knows this story (a Common Knowledge roll).

Every villain knows Nevermore was once the Raven, sidekick to the Owl. That legendary hero suffered a particularly bad reaction to Phobos' fear gas and fled—by pure accident—into a gang of common street thugs. One of the thugs brutally killed the Owl with a knife and became an instant celebrity among the super villain set. That thug was Carlos Ragsdale, and he's now one of Iron Head Tony's lieutenants.

Nevermore is notoriously elusive and canny. There's no telling where or when he'll strike, but the one piece of bait he isn't likely to resist is Ragsdale—if he can be coaxed out of the Red Hand's heavily protected compound.

If the villains are after the plutonium in the Ice Queen's gun, they'll need to capture or defeat Nevermore—a tale told in **Bring Me the Head of Nevermore!**, page 65.

LET 'EM EAT CANNOLI

Iron Head Tony sends a note or summons the villains for a special favor.

> *"That bastard K'lent. The one what's always droppin' stuff over the city to watch people fight over it. He's droppin' somethin' today. I want it.*
>
> *"Three p.m. today right in the middle of Central Park. The Loeb Boathouse. Bring it*

to me and I'll knock $25K off my price for the map. Capice?"

If the villains ask what's inside, Iron Head tells 'em to take a walk. He'll find someone else who "ain't such a Nosy Nelson." If they try to negotiate, they get one chance to make a Persuasion roll—at +2 if they mention the danger of the Green Hag. Success gets them $50K off the price of the map.

If the group isn't after the map, Iron Head offers $3,000 in store credit, or $5,000 with a successful Persuasion roll.

The drop does indeed take place at 3 p.m. sharp just as Tony says. Inside the drop crate is another box—iron and locked up tight with an electronic lock: Toughness 14, −4 to Knowledge (Electronics) to hack.

The Green Hag doesn't appear—don't roll an encounter—but Aileen the Burner does, and he brings five mutated alligator men with him!

- **Aileen the Burner:** See page 85.
- **Alligator Men (5):** See below.

ALLIGATOR MEN

These alligators were dumped into the lake sometime during the invasion. The Green Hag's dark magic has transformed them into terrifying servants.

Attributes: Agility d6, Smarts d4 (A), Spirit d8, Strength d12+2, Vigor d12+2

Skills: Fighting d10, Notice d6, Swimming d10

Pace: 6; **Parry:** 7; **Toughness:** 13 (3)

Special Abilities:

- **Aquatic:** Pace 10.
- **Armor +3:** Thick, scaly skin.
- **Attack, Melee:** Str+2d6. (Claws and teeth.)
- **Attack, Melee:** Str+d6. Reach +1. Minor Limitation (Can only attack foes to the rear) (Tail Lash.)
- **Size +1:** The gator men are seven feet tall and dense, and have a five-foot-long tail.

WHAT'S IN THE BOX?

If the villains return to Chelsea Piers with the box, the Red Hand escorts them directly to Iron Head. He opens the box with a combination he seems to know…and pulls out a box of fresh cannolis. He closes his eyes, takes a bite, and lets out a long sigh. He chews a long 30 seconds, then swallows.

"Good work, ya mooks. Now get outta here."

If the villains ask how he knew where the box would be, what was inside, and the combination, he just smiles and says "Dat's why I'm me and you're you. Now scram."

Iron Head won't reveal any more than that, but obviously he has some connection with to the outside world.

Under no circumstances does Tony share his cannolis.

NIGHT THING

Immediately after the villains defeat a group of gangers in Midtown, one of the survivors pleads for his life.

"Don't kill me! Don't kill me! I got something valuable…just lemme live and I'll show you!"

The thug's name is Louis. Assuming the characters let him live, he tells the following tale:

"Before all this crap went down I hung with the Griffin. Remember him? He was always trying to kill Guardian and always got his ass handed to him. But his last plan mighta worked. He found this old book somewhere then went to Iraq and dug up a statue. He called it something but me and the rest of the gang just called it the 'Night Thing.'

"I can show you where it's at. The book's there too! Anybody owns something like that gonna be somebody…and if you need a lieutenant…"

Louis is a normal Ganger (page 84). He's not a particularly good minion, nor is he especially loyal. If the villains agree to take him on or otherwise coerce him into showing them where Night Thing lies, he takes them about four blocks distant. From there he goes inside the ruins of an old department store (abandoned before the cordon) and points to a pile of rubble inside.

"Under that pile of concrete is one of the Griffin's hideouts, and that's where Night Thing is. Last I saw it was dormant—like a statue. Far as I know it's still there."

There are nearly three tons of concrete, rebar, and other rubble blocking the door to the basement. Between super strength and makeshift levers lying about, the team can move a ton every half-hour or so. If they keep a watch on the streets around them, nothing happens. If not, generate an encounter from the **Midtown Encounter Table** on page 40, or create one of your own. It's not wise to make that kind of noise and not set guards.

Once the rubble is clear, the group sees a stairway leading down into a dusty, cluttered basement filled with $10,000 in gold, silver, gems, jewels, and other precious metals, as well as a few paintings and sculptures. Obviously this was one of the Griffin's loot caches.

In the middle of the loot, starkly different from the otherwise mundane treasures that fill the room, is a nine-foot-tall, starkly terrifying statue. The thing is polished black stone and looks something like a standing gargoyle wrapped in leathery wings. Its face is mostly hidden, but what's visible is clearly something out of an ancient nightmare.

On a small table nearby is an ancient bundle of papyrus pages. On it are depictions of some terrible winged creature destroying entire cities with blasts of what must be fire or lightning. Words and symbols surround the drawing and fill the pages after. A Knowledge (Ancient History) test at −4 reveals the text to be the ancient Mesopotamian language of Akkadian. Scribbled directly on these priceless documents are the Griffin's hand-written notes, clearly legible in black Sharpie. They read:

- In the dark of night, say the words "Druaga Imhas!"
- The creature is pure destruction.
- It "wakes" for only 10 to 15 minutes.
- Only wakes once per century.

The instructions bear no further details but should be clear enough. Masterminds in the group should grok its purpose—it's a one-shot weapon capable of mass carnage and destruction.

If the villains attempt to wake the Night Thing during the day, nothing happens. If they follow the Griffin's instructions at night, the stone skin undulates and writhes with the sound of sundered stone. With a screeching howl from the depths of pre-history, the Night Thing lives!

The creature destroys anything and everything around it for the next 13 minutes. It is particularly drawn to fight any and all beings of power it sees.

The villains can transport the Night Thing to a location of their choosing and set it off like a living bomb. The statue weighs 600 pounds, but if it can be transported and awakened, it's a lethal weapon.

When it's 13 minutes of rage are over, the Night Thing's wings retract to cover its body. Seconds later, it is once again an immobile statue.

USING THE NIGHT THING

The Night Thing is a one-shot "gimme" for the villains. If it's used in the territory of a rival gang, it destroys dozens of their members (reducing Reputation by 1 during the **Gang War** Savage Tale, see page 68). If used against Neutron, the robot is defeated. Big Sis is too smart to stick around and fight it, even if the villains somehow lure her into its proximity when it wakes. It also can't break free of the cordon any more than anyone else. Otherwise, it's a powerful weapon the villains can use to do with as they please.

NIGHT THING

The creature is indeed an ancient demon of sorts, conjured up by ancient sorcerers at the dawn of recorded history. It's an incredibly powerful spirit of destruction. It primarily attacks with its massive fists, but can also emit a cone of scalding green fire that sears the flesh from most victims.

Attributes: Agility d10, Smarts d10, Spirit d10, Strength d12+6, Vigor d12

Skills: Fighting d12, Notice d10, Stealth d12+2

Cha: 0; **Pace:** 6; **Parry:** 8; **Toughness:** 18 (10)

Super Powers:

- **Armor +10:** Hardy. Heavy Armor.
- **Attack, Melee:** Damage Str+2d6, AP 4. Focus. Heavy Weapon. Lethal. Multiple Attacks.
- **Attack, Ranged:** Range 12/24/48, Damage 4d6. Cone. Heavy Weapon. Lethal.
- **Flight:** Pace 24, Climb 1, −1 to hit while flying.
- **Heightened Senses:** Low Light Vision.
- **Improved Frenzy:** The Night Thing can make two Fighting attacks in one round.

NEUTRON

Neutron misses his creator. His crude AI is just strong enough to know he's the one who killed her.

During the early days of the k'tharen invasion, the Gadgetress used her devices to fight the good fight. But the fins were tough opponents, so Gadgetress built her greatest creation yet—a super-powerful robot she named Neutron.

Gadgetress and Neutron turned the tide in New York City for a while. The pair drew the k'tharen away from the city to the forests farther north, allied with other avenging heroes, and defeated scores of the deadly invaders. Then came the v'sori treachery.

Gadgetress sensed something was wrong and didn't attend the victory celebrations. She survived the great betrayal and lived to fight for New York in the second wave of attacks. She and Neutron remained right up until the fight with OverBite and Iron Maiden, but probability and the chaos of battle eventually caught up with the duo. Neutron used his incredible eye beam to take down a v'sori mbuna. It crashed into a building and the resulting rubble fell onto Gadgetress.

The robot picked up his creator's broken body and staggered into the ruins of Lincoln Center. He sits there still, sitting on the stage, holding Gadgetress' bones in his iron lap.

THE SLEEPING GIANT

Neutron hibernates, but his sensors remain active. Scavengers have thoroughly looted the building around him, but anyone who comes within 30 feet or so of the robot runs when they see his single red eye begin scanning the room. The few who have attempted to touch, attack, or parley with the construct are still there—as piles of melted flesh and bone.

If Neutron is threatened further, he sets Gadgetress' bony corpse on the stage and attacks with robotic rage.

Taking out this very heavy threat requires planning and luck or it could easily result in the death of the entire party.

When and if Neutron is defeated, a rear panel can be cut open with a blowtorch and his two-pound chunk of uranium removed. Of course the party may want to use tongs and have a lead-lined box handy or risk **Radiation** poisoning! (See *Savage Worlds*.)

NEUTRON

Gadgetress was inspired by Gort from *The Day the Earth Stood Still* when she built Neutron, and he has the same basic appearance. He is also as powerful as the being that inspired his creation. His strength and durability are of cosmic level, and his eye beam can slice through even heavy tanks—at least when it's not damaged as it is right now.

Neutron does have one weakness. If he sees someone he believes is Gadgetress—perhaps due to a power or even someone putting on her costume (it's still on the corpse)—he's Stunned for d6 rounds while he processes

the information. After that, Neutron snaps out of it and becomes enraged, destroying anything in his path to get to whoever defiled his maker's memory.

Attributes: Agility d4, Smarts d8, Spirit d6, Strength d12+8, Vigor d12+4

Skills: Fighting d10, Notice d8, Shooting d12, Throwing d10

Pace: 8; **Parry:** 7; **Toughness:** 24 (8)

Special Abilities:

- **Armor +8:** Heavy Armor.
- **Attack, Melee:** Str+3d6, Heavy Weapon. (Claws and Teeth)
- **Attack, Ranged:** Range 24/48/96, Damage 3d10, RoF 1, AP 10, Heavy Weapon. Focus. Lethal. (Plasma Eye Beam) Neutron's eyebeams normally do 6d10 damage, but they were damaged in the fight and he has no one to repair them.
- **Construct:** +2 to recover from being Shaken; doesn't breathe; immune to disease and poison; ignores wound modifiers.
- **Heightened Senses:** Eagle Eyes. Infravision. Low Light Vision. Super Sense (Hearing).
- **Large:** Foes add +2 when attacking Neutron due to his large size.
- **Size +6:** Neutron stands 15 feet tall and is made of dense alloys.

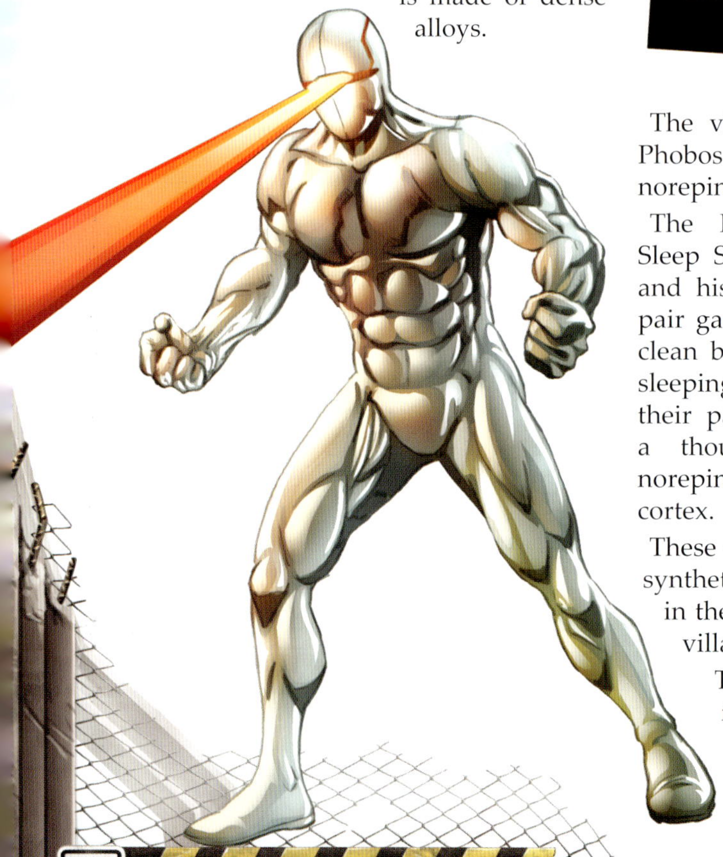

SCURVY DOGS

One of the villains' friends, such as Gervaise, is contracting rickets needs vitamin C. Or maybe the Consort asks for a basket of fresh fruit as payment for some information the group needs. Or maybe the villains themselves are Fatigued from a bad run of ration bars and need fresh food.

Vitamin C pills are nearly impossible to find now, even at the Red Hand's stores, so that leaves only one known source—the fruit trees in Central Park.

The team must take their chances if they want to help their friend. Let them go in and raid the place, and of course generate an encounter each time they do.

All together, the team needs about $1,000 worth of fresh food to stave off whatever condition they're fighting. Use the **Central Park Encounters** (page 42) and the information under **Grasping Vines & Forbidden Fruit** on page 41.

THIS IS YOUR BRAIN ON FEAR

The villains are likely here because Dr. Phobos told them they could find synthesized norepinephrine in the labs.

The Malidore Institute for Advanced Sleep Studies was a front for Dr. Phobos and his partner, Dr. Elijah Malidore. The pair gave homeless people hot food and a clean bed in exchange for "studying their sleeping patterns." In truth, they drugged their patients, magnified their nightmares a thousand-fold, and withdrew their norepinephrine direct from their cerebral cortex.

These enhanced samples eventually led to synthetic versions, some of which remain in the facility and can be retrieved by the villains.

The Malidore Institute is on the top floor of a 10-story building and has remained relatively untouched—because something still roams its upper corridors. The elevator doesn't work so most villains must use the stairs. They are littered with food wrappers, dented cans, soda bottles, and other refuse—likely gathered from the surrounding convenience stores in the early days of the cordon.

THINGS FROM NIGHTMARES

Malidore and Phobos continued their experiments and extractions right up until New York City lost electricity. The last surge of power slammed into their fear-induction system and turned their final crop of patients into literal zombies—one of which also developed latent super powers!

Read the following as the party emerges from the stairwell (or the elevator if they choose to climb up the shaft).

You emerge into a lobby. Clearly this was once a clean space for people waiting on medical service, but it's been trashed. Food containers and water bottles lie everywhere and the couches are overturned and their cushions ripped to shreds. Wind whips through the broken plate glass windows, stirring up the trash and obscuring strange sounds in the distant, dark spaces beyond.

A number of doors lead off the lobby, including a set of double doors with smashed glass panes leading into what was obviously some sort of control room. Another door leads to a large and impressive office, and still more lead off into dark hallways.

THE OFFICE COMPLEX

The entire floor is a trash pile of empty food and beverage containers and human waste. The place smells like a cross between a

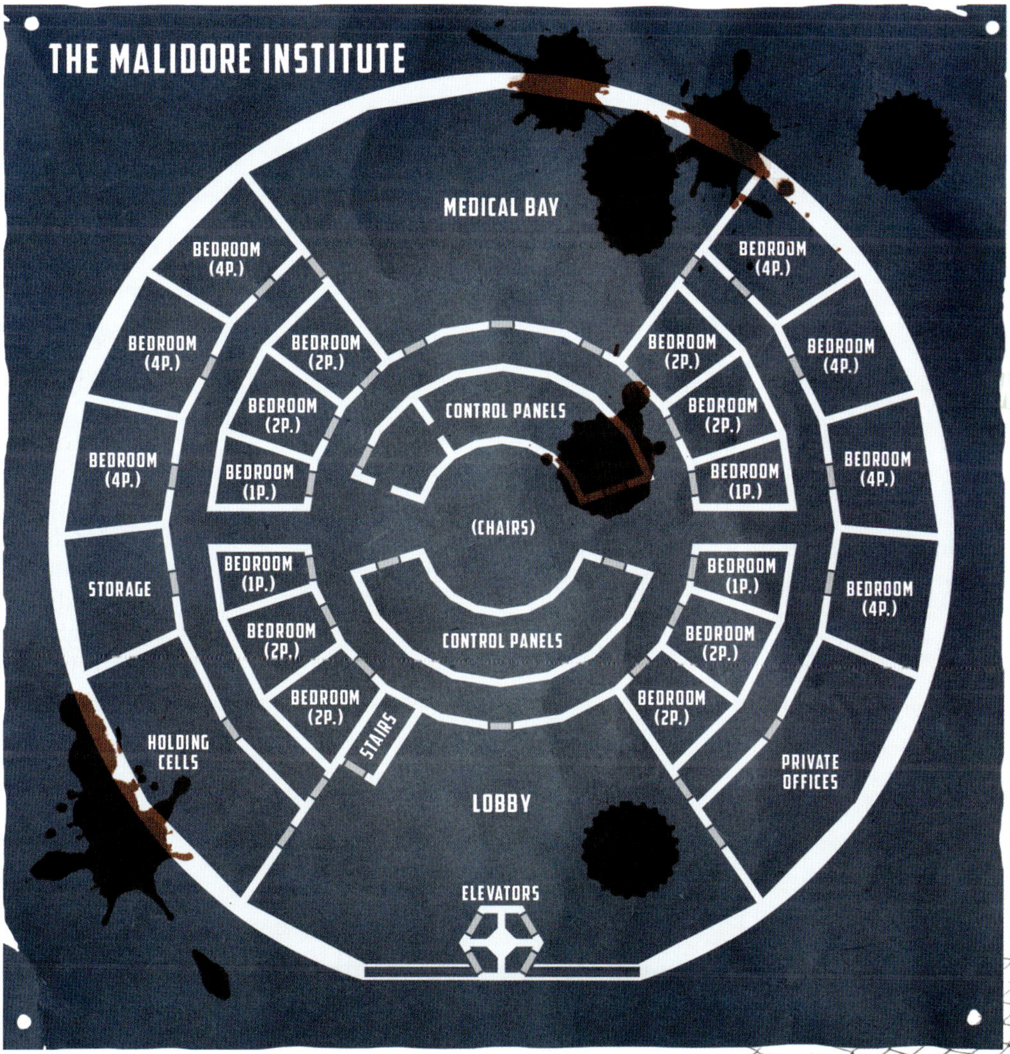

sewer and an abattoir, and given there are no windows except in the lobby, is perpetually dark no matter what time of day the villains visit.

Control Room: Dr. Malidore and Dr. Phobos watched the victims here and could actually project fuzzy visions of their worst nightmares on their screens.

Dr. Malidore's Office: This once-lavish room had a glass desk complete with holo-screen, though it now lies in bloody shards on the lush red carpet. Once mounted on the walls, numerous abstract paintings of super heroes and villains lie strewn about the room.

Dr. Malidore's files are scattered about as well. A quick glance at them reveals very little information—basic height, weight, and stated fear (spiders, drowning, etc.). Anyone with a medical background realizes the information is woefully incomplete. (Dr. Malidore wasn't interested in anything besides the patient's fears, and enough bio-data to guess at anesthesia.)

Bedrooms: This is where the patients were put to sleep, then strapped to their beds. Some of the leather bonds bear teeth marks where the victims chewed their way through.

Medical Bay: Like the other rooms in the institute, the medical bay is a wreck. Bloodstains smear the floor but there are no corpses (the blood is from unfortunate scavengers who ventured here looking for salvage—and drugs). Gurneys lie on their side amid piles of unopened syringes, tanks of anesthesia or oxygen, and medical equipment such as heart monitors and hand-held X-ray machines (none of which work without electricity, of course).

Standing against the far wall is a horde of men and women in ragged, bloody patient's gowns. Play this one for creeps. The patients remain stock still as the intruders enter the room. If they get near or make a noise, one of them, a slim figure with pale blonde hair, slowly turns her rotting face toward the intruders and screams!

This individual is Sabrina Reischl—but the villains will come to call her *Nightmare!*

The round after Sabrina screams, the rest of the "wretches" turn and follow suit with a terrifying hiss. There are 17 of the things so they swarm over the villains like rats. They've also been here long enough to know how to circle around through the various hallways and attack from behind!

Sabrina proves especially deadly. She uses her *intangibility* to fade in and out of the horde, attacking the intruders in terrifying "fly-by" attacks. Her sudden, unearthly screams and the wailing of the wretches should make for a truly horrifying battle.

The prize is in sight, however. In the far right corner of the room is a rack of vials, many of which remain intact. Inside is a viscous, snot-colored goop clearly labeled norepinephrine.

NIGHTMARE

Sabrina Reischl was a powerful telepath before she perished here in Dr. Malidore's facility. She has become even more powerful in undeath.

Attributes: Agility d10, Smarts d4 (A), Spirit d12, Strength d8, Vigor d6

Skills: Fighting d10, Notice d6, Shooting d10, Throwing d10

Cha: −2; **Pace:** 6; **Parry:** 7; **Toughness:** 7

Hindrances: Distinctive Appearance (Undead), Mania (Major—psychotic)

Edges: Alertness, Dead Shot

Gear: —

Super Powers:

- **Attack, Ranged:** Range 12/24/48, Damage 4d6, Cone (only) (Banshee wail.)
- **Awareness:** Nightmare can sense everything around her, even through most obstacles. This negates the Gang Up bonus.
- **Damage Field:** Anyone standing next to Nightmare suffers horrific visions of their own worst fears.
- **Fear:** Nightmare's *fear* power is contingent on her ranged attack.
- **Flight:** Nightmare can fly at up to twice her walking Pace.
- **Intangibility:** Phase. Nightmare can pass through walls and other solid objects at will. She can use her powers while *intangible* with a Spirit roll via the Phase modifier.
- **Telekinesis:** Nightmare can move items with a gesture at Strength 10.
- **Undead:** +2 Toughness; +2 to recover from Shaken; doesn't breathe; immune to disease & poison; no additional damage from called shots; ignore 1 level of wound penalties; −2 Charisma.

WRETCHES

The wretches are tortured souls driven mad by Dr. Malidore's fear inducer. Sallow-skinned, their hair is long and stringy (or falling out) and their eyes are cloudy and vacant. Most are covered in sores, wounds, or scabs and look like zombies from a bad horror movie. They lived for quite a while here but eventually passed. They remain animated *only* as long as Nightmare remains conscious. If she is Incapacitated or destroyed, they fall…never to rise again.

Attributes: Agility d6, Smarts d4 (A), Spirit d6, Strength d6, Vigor d6
Skills: Fighting d6, Notice d4
Cha: –4; **Pace:** 6; **Parry:** 5; **Toughness:** 7
Hindrances: Ugly
Edges: —
Gear: —
Special Abilities:

- **Claws:** Str+d6. Their claws glow with violet psychic energy.
- **Undead:** +2 Toughness; +2 to recover from Shaken; doesn't breathe; immune to disease & poison; no additional damage from called shots; ignore 1 level of wound penalties; –2 Charisma.

SAFE AT LAST

This tale begins with a deadly fright and ends in tragedy. Pick a character who has any kind of "devil" or hellish motif. If none do, choose the one with the lowest Charisma. Don't choose a flyer—that will ruin the fun.

The villain is poised on a rooftop or ledge somewhere in the city, late at night. He and his companions might be watching their foes or scouting for new locations to scavenge. Suddenly he feels a cold chill creep up his spine. He senses something behind him and turns—just in time to see a screeching phantom appear from the darkness! The thing pushes hard—with a Strength of d12+2—and tries to knock the chosen criminal off the rooftop. Make an opposed roll. If the phantom wins, the victim must make a Fear test as he flies off the roof.

Unless the Game Master knows how high up the character is, the height is d20 stories. If none of the other villains have any way of saving their comrade—via swinging, stretching, flying, or the like—he gets a chance to grab a flag pole this time. It's a simple Agility roll, so he should make it. The point is to scare him—not kill him.

The phantom disappears after that and doesn't reappear that night.

FAMILIARITY BREEDS CONTEMPT

Soon after, the spirit returns. This time it doesn't push anyone though—it simply emerges from the darkness, screams, and vanishes. The villains must make a Fear test each time, but everyone who sees it also gets a Common Knowledge roll at –4. Any characters who were natives of New York roll at –2 instead, and those who were involved with organized crime ignore the penalty all together. Should anyone make it, they think the phantom looks something like the daughter of Yuri Petrenko—one of the most powerful Russian mob bosses. A raise recalls the girl's name was Irena.

The spirit haunts her chosen victim for a week or so, only at night, and usually when he least expects it. She is completely non-corporeal. Magic or similar types of powers can affect her, but even if Incapacitated she returns. She can't be talked to, reasoned with, or captured.

The spirit is indeed Irena Petrenko, daughter of Yuri Petrenko, and though she's insane—and dead—she's looking for help.

If the party pays attention, they might note that her appearances are actually leading them to a 5th Avenue high-rise. The villains might also decide to search for Yuri's home or office on their own—a Streetwise roll at –2 turns up the address.

The Streetwise roll or the villains' memory eventually recalls a bit more about Yuri. Namely, that he was the New York City boss of the Russian mafia, and was the archenemy of a super hero called the Hellion. The two battled for over a decade, but since both operated in the shadows it was rarely public news. Still, anyone who knew the New York crime scene knew of their epic struggle. Yuri had revealed Hellion's identity and killed one of his girlfriends. Hellion stuck to the foolish code of the world's heroes though, and even though he brought Yuri down time after time only to see him released by crooked attorneys, cops, and judges, he still wouldn't kill him.

THE DEVIL'S DUE

When the group eventually gets to Petrenko's high-rise, it's full of gangers and scav squatters on every floor. The Game Master can make the group run the gauntlet if desired—with Irena turning up at the worst possible times—or you can cut to the chase. Read the following when they finally get to Petrenko's office.

You reach double doors that must lead to the mafia boss's office. Two corpses lie long-dead to either side, submachine guns still in their hands with not a shot fired. The symbol of a devil's trident has been burned into the wall above them—Hellion's symbol.

You open the doors to see what looks like a war zone. Papers, books, and artwork lie everywhere. A massive aquarium has been shattered and its unfortunate occupants lie long dead on the plush carpet. Couches are ripped, bullet casings are plentiful, and there are blood spatters on the floor, walls, and even the ceiling.

But what really catches your attention is the shattered glass desk at the center of the room and the immense corpse of Yuri Petrenko lying across it. Driven into his back is a samurai sword—hilt deep.

Only bulletproof glass spared the windows. Everything else is a wreck. A shelf of rare sculptures and other treasures lies on its side and glass from the desk and several mirrors lies everywhere.

The sword is *not* a trademark weapon of Hellion, but a Common Knowledge roll remembers that it was the weapon of the assassin Petrenko hired to kill Hellion's wife.

Closer examination reveals the big man was beaten furiously before he died, and marks on his hands and knuckles hint that he gave as well as he got before losing the final showdown.

A Notice roll also reveals the calendar on his desk last marked three days before the cordon. It seems Hellion—with nothing left to lose—took his final revenge before fleeing the city.

The sculptures and other objets d'art are worth a total of $250,000 to the Red Hand.

SAFE AT LAST

As the villains look over the scene and gather the treasures, they hear a light cry from the closet—the one blocked by the fallen bookcase. When they open the door, they see only the corpse of Irena sitting on the floor, hugging a doll. Her father hid her in the closet when he heard Hellion approaching and she remained trapped in there after his death. She starved and her spirit has been looking for someone to "free" her ever since.

On the plus side, the time-lock safe in the wall of the closet is wide open. Inside is $10,000,000 in cash (worth $100K to the Red Hand), a gold-plated .45 pistol and two magazines with 7 rounds each (total value $10K, but only to Iron Head Tony), and a dossier containing all the personal information on Hellion (and several other heroes, politicians, and even villains).

Once found, Irena's spirit slips away into the ether and haunts the villains no more.

A WING & A SCARE

Skye Briggs, one of Donald Bowers' Buzzards and former girlfriend, is tired of his caution. She thinks the gang should rule the streets as well as the rooftops and has led a mini-revolt to prove it.

At some point after the villains have salvaged some valuable item or looted a foe, the buzzards drop stun grenades on the villains and swoop in to take their ill-gotten gains.

Twice the number of villains (led by Skye, who's a Wild Card) swoop down from the sky. Half grab the goods while the others tangle with any villains who resisted the stun grenades for a round. A few might also run interference if their prey can also fly.

Their goal is to shake off any pursuers, so they attempt to sabotage any flight-based equipment, render flying foes unconscious, or simply lead them away while the ones with the goods make their escape.

If the Buzzards are successful, they fly off with the stolen loot. Finding one of their aeries requires a cunning plan, scouring the rooftops, or a talk with someone like Gervaise (page 84).

ROGUES GALLERY

BLOCKBUSTER

Jake Reed was part of a team called the Fabulous Five, a reality-hopping band of super heroes before the v'sori invasion. He was the mechanic and repairman of the group before he was transormed by exposure to strange elements in some distant dimension.

As Blockbuster, he's a tall, wide figure of living gray pavement with fists that can wreck foundations!

Attributes: Agility d8, Smarts d6, Spirit d10, Strength d12+8, Vigor d12+6

Skills: Boating d6, Climbing d8, Driving d8, Fighting d10, Gambling, d6, Healing d6, Intimidation d10, Knowledge (Mechanical Engineering) d6, Notice d6, Persuasion d4, Piloting d8, Repair d10, Shooting d6, Streetwise d8, Survival (Urban) d8, Swimming d6, Taunt d10, Throwing d10

Cha: +2; **Pace:** 6; **Parry:** 8; **Toughness:** 25 (8)

Hindrances: Code of Honor, Distinctive Appearance (massive body made of living concrete), Heroic, Loyal

Edges: Block, Charismatic, Combat Reflexes, Counterattack, Elan, Harder to Kill, Improvisational Fighter, Mighty Blow, Improved Nerves of Steel, Improved Sweep

Gear: —

Special Abilities:

- **Armor +8:** Hardy. Heavy Armor. (Concrete skin.)
- **Attack, Melee:** Damage Str+ 5d6. Focus. (Fists)
- **Earthquake:** Earthshake. (Blockbuster slams his fists into the pavement or ground.)
- **Regeneration:** Blockbuster rolls to regenerate every minute. Regrowth.
- **Size +1:** Blockbuster is eight feet tall.
- **Super Attribute:** Strength +9. Vigor +8
- **Toughness +5:** Blockbuster is as tough as they come.

THE BUZZARDS

THE BUZZARD

Donald Bowers is an ordinary guy with the ability to fly and some very minor fighting skill. He knows that, and does his best to avoid direct fights with the other factions in the NYCP. It's a smart strategy that has kept him alive so far, but his gang sees him as timid.

Donald's preferred tactic is to drop stun grenades on his victims from above, swoop in to take their stuff, then depart before they can retaliate.

Attributes: Agility d8, Smarts d10, Spirit d8, Strength d6, Vigor d6

Skills: Climbing d8, Driving d6, Fighting d6, Healing d6, Intimidation d4, Investigation d8, Knowledge (Engineering) d10, Notice d8, Persuasion d6, Piloting d10, Repair d12, Stealth d10, Streetwise d6, Survival (Urban) d8, Throwing d6

Cha: 0; **Pace:** 6; **Parry:** 5; **Toughness:** 7 (2)
Hindrances: Cautious, Greedy (Minor)
Edges: Alertness, Improved Frenzy
Gear: Insulated suit (+2) and helmet (+4), 2× frag grenades (Range 5/10/20, Damage 3d6).
Special Abilities:
- **Attack, Melee:** Damage Str+d6, AP 2. Device (Electro-talons).
- **Flight:** Pace 24, Climb 1, −1 to hit while flying.
- **Heightened Senses:** Low Light Vision. Device (Night Vision Helmet).
- **Stun:** Device. Area Effect (LBT). Strong. (Stun grenades.)

BUZZARD

Donald Bowers' thugs are not loyal or grateful. They see him as a weak and timid leader, but the only one who knows how to acquire and repair the tech that gives them their names.

Attributes: Agility d6, Smarts d6, Spirit d6, Strength d6, Vigor d6
Skills: Climbing d6, Driving d6, Fighting d6, Intimidation d4, Notice d8, Piloting d8, Repair d4, Shooting d6, Stealth d8, Streetwise d6, Survival (Urban) d6, Swimming d4, Taunt d8, Throwing d6
Cha: 0; **Pace:** 6; **Parry:** 5; **Toughness:** 8 (2)
Hindrances: Arrogant, Greedy
Edges: Alertness, Frenzy
Gear: Insulated suit (+2) and helmet (+4). A few occasionally carry rifles they use to snipe the rooftops, but Donald discourages it, believing deadly force encourages deadly retaliation.
Super Powers
- **Attack, Melee:** Damage Str+2d6, AP 2. Device (Electro-talons, Mk II).
- **Flight:** Pace 24, Climb 1, −1 to hit while flying.
- **Heightened Senses:** Low Light Vision. Device (Night Vision Helmet).

CHEM HOUNDS

Pollution and chemical runoff have mutated some of the larger canines left behind into feral dogs the locals call chem hounds. Green acid oozes from their dripping fangs, allowing them to bite through most armor.

Attributes: Agility d8, Smarts d6 (A), Spirit d8, Strength d10, Vigor d10
Skills: Fighting d10, Notice d8, Stealth d10
Pace: 8; **Parry:** 7; **Toughness:** 9(2)
Special Abilities:
- **Armor +2:** Leathery hide.
- **Acid Bite:** Str+d8, AP 2.
- **Go For the Throat:** With a raise on the attack roll, the chemical hounds hit the defender's least armored spot.

THE CONSORT

Riya Dubashi was a counter-intelligence operative for the CIA before the invasion, and one of their best. She was discovered by one of the super villains she captured in a long game of cat and mouse and beaten nearly to death. Riya recovered but faded into the shadows, trusting *no one* to guard her identity but herself.

Since the invasion, she's gone to work for none other than…Dr. Destruction! She has a fusion generator in her subterranean base for power and can occasionally get satellite signals past the v'sori sensors to contact the doctor. (Riya has also deduced his *true* identity—see *Necessary Evil*.)

Attributes: Agility d4, Smarts d12, Spirit d10, Strength d6, Vigor d6

Skills: Driving d4, Fighting d4, Healing d10, Investigation d12, Knowledge (Electronics) d12, Knowledge (Computers) d12, Notice d12, Repair d10, Stealth d10, Swimming d4

Cha: 0; **Pace:** 4; **Parry:** 4; **Toughness:** 5

Hindrances: Heroic, Lame, Loyal, Vow (Major—save the world!)

Edges: Alertness, Jack of All Trades, Scholar

Gear: A hidden basement of computers. She can tap directly into any existing lines to power them up, turn them on, and monitor whatever they were designed to see. This is a very limited operation to keep her from being detected, so she has to choose a handful of specific cameras, ATMs, or other devices to monitor at any given time. Also, many areas of the city aren't covered anymore due to the damage.

DR. PHOBOS

Phobos' Fear gun is empty, but he keeps one fear grenade on him for emergencies.

Attributes: Agility d8, Smarts d12, Spirit d10, Strength d6, Vigor d6

Skills: Driving d6, Fighting d8, Healing d8, Intimidation d10, Knowledge (Chemistry) d12, Knowledge (Medicine) d12, Knowledge (Psychiatry) d10, Notice d10, Persuasion d8, Repair d8, Shooting d8, Streetwise d8, Stealth d8, Taunt d10, Throwing d8

Cha: –2; **Pace:** 6; **Parry:** 6; **Toughness:** 5

Hindrances: Cautious, Mania (Major: obsession with fear), Quirk (Usually works alone)

Edges: Alertness, Combat Reflexes, Elan, Improved Level Headed, Scholar, Strong Willed

Gear: Fear grenade (see **Chemistry 1001** (page 50).

Special Abilities:

- **Attack, Ranged:** Device. Cone only. (Fear gun).
- **Fear:** Device. Terror. Projectile. Contingent on Attack, Ranged (Fear gun).

THE FIXER

The Fixer is elderly, but she still knows how to pull a trigger.

Attributes: Agility d6, Smarts d12, Spirit d8, Strength d4, Vigor d6

Skills: Fighting d6, Healing d6, Intimidation d8, Investigation d8, Knowledge (Chemistry) d8, Knowledge (Electronics) d10, Knowledge (Engineering) d10, Lockpicking d6, Notice d8, Persuasion d6, Repair d12, Shooting d8, Stealth d6, Streetwise d8, Throwing d6

Cha: 0; **Pace:** 5; **Parry:** 5; **Toughness:** 5

Hindrances: Elderly, Quirk (cat lover), Vengeful (Minor)

Edges: Jack-of-All-Trades, Level Headed, McGyver, Mr. Fix It, Scholar

Gear: The Fixer has access to armor and weapons of all types.

Special Abilities:

- **Interface:** Device. Code breaker.
- **Invent:** Level 5. On The Fly.
- **Malfunction:** Device. Area effect.

FULL AUTO

Glenn Wein was a world-class competitive gamer before the war. He had never actually fired a real weapon til the k'tharen came. Then he got into shape, joined the special forces, and stayed on through the v'sori invasion and the fall of New York. Now he's the city most vigilant—and violent—protector.

Attributes: Agility d10, Smarts d10, Spirit d10, Strength d10, Vigor d10

Skills: Driving d10, Fighting d12, Intimidation d12, Investigation d8, Lockpicking d8, Notice d10, Shooting d12, Stealth d10, Throwing d8

Cha: –2; **Pace:** 6; **Parry:** 10; **Toughness:** 12(4)

Hindrances: Heroic, Mean, Vow (Major—protect the weak, kill the wicked)

Edges: Alertness, Assassin, Improved Block, Brawler, Combat Reflexes, Improved Counterattack, Danger Sense, Dead Shot, Improved Dodge, Extraction, Improved First Strike, Harder to Kill, Improved Level Headed, Marksman, Martial Artist, Quick, Tough as Nails, Two-Fisted.

Gear: Body armor (+4, –4 AP), a variety of regular weapons and grenades with plenty of ammo. He particularly likes his Barret .50 cal sniper rifle as it lets him take out most threats at a distance (Range 50/100/200, Damage 2d10, AP 4, RoF 1).

GANGERS

Some of these thugs were gang members before the fall of New York. Some joined after out of desire or necessity. All are aggressive, territorial, and itching for a fight.

There's one Gang Leader for every dozen Gangers.

Loot: Roll a d6 × $10 per member of the group if defeated, cowed, or robbed. The total is the amount of scavenged valuables they have on them in dollars. Seven gangers, for example, have 7d6 × $10 in goods on their person, split between them.

GANGER

These are the standard run-of-the-mill thugs. The Game Master should spice them up with a little personality when encountered. One might be mouthy, one might be larger with a higher Strength, one might have found a blaster pistol, and so on.

Attributes: Agility d6, Smarts d4, Spirit d6, Strength d6, Vigor d6

Skills: Climbing d4, Driving d6, Fighting d6, Gambling d4, Intimidation d6, Notice d6, Persuasion d4, Shooting d4, Stealth d6, Survival (Urban) d4, Taunt d6, Throwing d4

Cha: –2; **Pace:** 6; **Parry:** 5; **Toughness:** 5

Hindrances: Greedy (Minor), Mean

Edges: —

Gear: 9mm pistol (Range 12/24/48, Damage 2d6, RoF 1, SA) with only 1d6 bullets, iron pipe (Str+d6). Some occasionally have other weapons as well.

GANG LEADER

These are the slightly craftier, more dangerous thugs the other low-lifes have agreed to listen to. For now, anyway.

The statistics below are common, but the GM should consider an additional Edge, piece of gear, and/or personality trait to make them more memorable.

Attributes: Agility d6, Smarts d6, Spirit d8, Strength d6, Vigor d6

Skills: Fighting d8, Notice d6, Persuastion d6, Shooting d6, Stealth d6, Streetwise d8

Cha: –2; **Pace:** 6; **Parry:** 6; **Toughness:** 5

Hindrances: Greedy (Minor), Mean

Edges: Gang leaders have three Combat Edges, often including Block, Combat Reflexes, First Strike, or Trademark Weapon.

Gear: Scavenged M16A4 (Range 24/48/96, Damage 2d8, AP 2, RoF 3) with one full 20-round magazine and heavy pipe (Str+d6). Most carry at least one frag grenade as well (Range 5/10/20, Damage 3d6).

GERVAISE

Neighborhood snitch Gervaise uses standard statistics for a Scavenger (page 90), but has a knack for rumors (Streetwise d12). A visit with Gervaise and $20 in goods gets the scoop on most current events. More serious dirt requires a much larger payment, or Intimidation.

GOLDEN GAL

Tawanda Jones was always told what she *couldn't* do growing up in Harlem. But her family always believed and supported her and she eventually became one of the foremost inventors of her age. Despite the tragedy of losing her "family," the Fabulous Five, during the fall of New York, Tawanda has soldiered on, battling for the weak in her amazing golden power armor.

Attributes: Agility d8, Smarts d12+2, Spirit d10, Strength d12+6, Vigor d6

Skills: Driving d6, Fighting d10, Healing d10, Intimidation d10, Knowledge (Mechanical Engineering) d12, Notice d10, Persuasion d8, Piloting d10, Repair d12, Shooting d10, Streetwise d8, Survival (Urban) d8, Swimming d6, Taunt d6, Throwing d10

Cha: +2; **Pace:** 6; **Parry:** 7; **Toughness:** 15 (10)

Hindrances: Code of Honor, Heroic, Loyal

Edges: Attractive, Combat Reflexes, Elan, Marksman, Hard to Kill, McGyver, Mrs. Fix It

Gear: —

Special Abilities:

- **Armor +10:** Device. Heavy Armor. (Golden power suit.)
- **Attack, Ranged:** Range 24/48/96, Damage 5d6, AP 6, RoF 1. Cone. Focus. Heavy Weapon.
- **Attack, Melee:** Str+3d6. Focus. Heavy Weapon. Stackable. (Arm servos.)
- **Broadcast:** Device. (Wireless electronics suite.)
- **Danger Sense:** Device. (Sensor suite and warning system.)
- **Damage Field:** Damage 3d6. Device. Medium Template. Selective. (Force blast, always non-lethal.)
- **Flight:** Pace 48, Climb 2, –2 to be hit while flying.

• **Heightened Senses:** Device. Eagle Eyes. Infravision. Low Light Vision. Spatial Sense. (Sensor Suite.)
• **Interface:** Tawanda's suit can interface with most any type of electronics.
• **Stun:** Projectile. Contingent on successful Shooting attack. Device. (Chest mounted stun ray.)
• **Super Attribute:** Strength +8.

THE GREEN HAG & MINIONS

The arch nemesis of hero Allan Fate is actually the ghost of a witch named Irnan. She is served by a goblin called Aileen the Burner and two phantom hounds, Bran and Sceolong.

The hag and her hounds dwell just outside the material world, appearing only when encountered or a significant ruckus is raised somewhere in Central Park. Aileen the Burner is physical, however, and lives in the Loeb Boathouse—now a disgusting lair of filth, bones, and debris.

THE GREEN HAG

Ancient Irnan remains in this world to torment the living. She uses her magic to fill the park with succulent fruits to lure in trespassers, then savages them with her dark magic or baying hounds. The "witch" only has a small repertoire of spells in her ghostly form, listed below as super powers.

Attributes: Agility d6, Smarts d10, Spirit d10, Strength d10, Vigor d8
Skills: Fighting d6, Notice d10, Shooting d10, Stealth d10, Taunt d12
Cha: –4; **Pace:** 6; **Parry:** 5; **Toughness:** 6
Hindrances: Mean, Ugly
Edges: —
Special Abilities:
• **Attack, Ranged:** Range 12/24/48, Damage 4d6. Cone. (Sorcerous green fire.)
• **Ethereal:** Irnan is a ghost and can only be affected by magic or iron.
• **Flight:** 4× Pace.–1 to hit. Climb 2.
• **Invisibility:** –6 to hit. Irnan can appear or disappear at will.
• **Telekinesis:** Range 12", Strength d12+2. Focus. Heavy Weapon.
• **Undying:** Irnan can be defeated (Incapacitated) but returns each night unless she is slain with the weapon of Finn MacCool, which isn't in the city. While she is gone from this world, the trees in Central Park return to normal and do not bear fruit or vegetables.

AILEEN THE BURNER

Aileen is a short but stout goblin who breathes fire. The witch Irnan has enslaved him to her service for thousands of years.

Attributes: Agility d10, Smarts d8, Spirit d10, Strength d12, Vigor d10
Skills: Climbing d8, Fighting d6, Intimidation d12, Notice d6, Shooting d10, Stealth d12, Survival d10, Taunt d10, Throwing d10
Cha: –6; **Pace:** 6; **Parry:** 6; **Toughness:** 7
Hindrances: Bloodthirsty, Mean
Edges: Acrobat, Strong Willed
Gear: —
Special Abilities:
• **Attack, Ranged:** Range 12/24/48, Damage 4d6. Cone. (Fiery breath.)

THE HOUNDS

These hounds once served the ancient hero Finn MacCool of Irish legend. Their spirits were taken by his enemy, Irnan, and corrupted long ago.

Attributes: Agility d10, Smarts d6 (A), Spirit d10, Strength d12+2, Vigor d10
Skills: Fighting d10, Notice d10, Stealth d10
Pace: 8; **Parry:** 7; **Toughness:** 11 (4)
Special Abilities:
• **Armor +4:** Leathery hide covered in ghostly iron chains.
• **Improved Frenzy:** The dogs make two Fighting attacks per round at no penalty.
• **Ghostly Bite:** Str+d8, AP 8.
• **Go For the Throat:** With a raise on the attack roll, the hounds hit the defender's least armored spot.
• **Ethereal:** The ghostly dogs can only be affected by magic or iron.
• **Undying:** If a hound is slain it returns the following night.

HARLEM KNIGHTS

The Knights are truly the NYCP's last remaining force for good. They're made up of around 1,000 Gangers and 2,000 Scavengers. Replace the Ganger and Gang Leader's Hindrances with Loyal.

The gang also has two armored school buses, three armored cars and a single black Yaschuk (see page 16).

Every 10 Gangers have one Gang Leader, and a super-powered being. Really important operations might mean Nevermore tags along, and sometimes Full Auto watches the group from on high as well (though he is never invited).

HENRY JONES

The leader of the Harlem Knigths has no super powers, but his integrity and shrewd wit have found him many loyal followers.

Attributes: Agility d8, Smarts d10, Spirit d12, Strength d10, Vigor d10

Skills: Driving d8, Fighting d8, Healing d8, Intimidation d8, Investigation d6, Knowledge (Fire Fighting) d8, Notice d8, Persuastion d6, Repair d4, Shooting d6, Stealth d6, Streetwise d8, Throwing d6

Cha: 0; **Pace:** 6; **Parry:** 7; **Toughness:** 7

Hindrances: Heroic, Pacifist (Minor), Stubborn, Vow (Major—protect and preserve New York until the invasion is over)

Edges: Alertness, Block, Brave, Bruiser, Command, Command Presence, Counterattack, Extraction, Giant Killer, Hard to Kill, Hold the Line!, Leader of Men, Improved Level Headed, Mighty Blow, Natural Leader, Improved Sweep, Trademark Weapon (sledgehammer—Gertie).

Gear: Streetsweeper with rubber bullets (Range 12/24/48, Damage 1–3d6), sledge hammer (Str+d10).

K'THAREN

The "fins" are an amphibious race combining the jagged teeth of sharks with the scaly skin of crocodiles. Most stand over seven feet tall and are as strong as elephants. Armed with advanced armor and weaponry they are a match for most of Earth's super-powered beings.

COMMANDER

The most vicious k'tharen are cybernetically enhanced to be even *more* dangerous. They also receive some basic command training, but mostly they are valued for their pure ferocity.

Attributes: Agility d10, Smarts d8, Spirit d10, Strength d12+4, Vigor d12+1

Skills: Driving d8, Fighting d12, Intimidation d12, Notice d10, Shooting d12, Swimming d10, Throwing d8

Cha: –6; **Pace:** 10; **Parry:** 8; **Toughness:** 17 (6)

Hindrances: Bloodthirsty, Mean

Edges: Combat Reflexes, Command, Fervor, Improved Frenzy

Gear: Combat armor (+6, –4 AP), 4× fusion grenades (Range 5/10/20, Damage 3d8, AP 2), pulse rifle (Range 20/40/80, Damage 3d6, AP 4, RoF 1).

Special Abilities:

- **Aquatic:** Pace 10.
- **Bite/Claws:** Str+d8.
- **Pain Reduction:** This cybernetic implant allows them to ignore up to two points of wound penalties.
- **Size +3:** K'tharen commanders tend to be the largest of their species.
- **Weapon Link:** When using their issued pulse rifle, the K'tharen commander may ignore 2 points of penalties to their Shooting rolls.

MUTATE

The v'sori scientist M'oro is attempting to create a new species of k'tharen called a "tharn" (see below). This has produced a large number of unfortunate, mutated test subjects.

Attributes: Agility d8, Smarts d4(A), Spirit d8, Strength d12+2, Vigor d12

Skills: Fighting d8, Intimidation d12, Notice d4, Swimming d10, Throwing d6

Cha: –6; **Pace:** 7; **Parry:** 6; **Toughness:** 10

Hindrances: Bloodthirsty, Mean

Edges: Berserk, Improved Frenzy

Gear: —.

Special Abilities:

- **Aquatic:** Pace 10.
- **Attack, Melee:** Damage Str+2d6, AP 2. (Psionic bite / claw.)
- **Bite/Claws:** Str+d6.
- **Size +2:** Mutates are hulking figures of twisted flesh and muscle.

WARRIOR

K'tharen warriors, often called "fins" or "shark troopers," were one of the v'sori's most dangerous foes. They were conqured only when the alien overlords promised them galaxies of strange beings to battle—and devour—if they would serve the Overmind.

Attributes: Agility d8, Smarts d6, Spirit d8, Strength d12+2, Vigor d10

Skills: Driving d6, Fighting d10, Intimidation d10, Notice d8, Shooting d10,

Swimming d10, Throwing d8
Cha: –6; **Pace:** 7; **Parry:** 7; **Toughness:** 15 (6)
Hindrances: Bloodthirsty, Mean
Edges: Combat Reflexes, Improved Frenzy
Gear: Combat armor (+6, –4 AP), 2× fusion grenades (Range 5/10/20, Damage 3d8, AP 2), pulse rifle (Range 20/40/80, Damage 3d6, AP 4, RoF 1).
Special Abilities:
- **Aquatic:** Pace 10.
- **Bite/Claws:** Str+d6.
- **Size +2:** Fin troopers are eight feet of rage and hate.

THARN (K'THAREN SUPER SOLDIERS)

M'oro's new breed of k'tharen are on par with k'tharen commanders but without the implants. More importantly, they've been bred to resist the psionic powers of the v'sori—including the Overmind!

Attributes: Agility d8, Smarts d6, Spirit d8, Strength d12+4, Vigor d10
Skills: Driving d6, Fighting d10, Intimidation d10, Notice d8, Shooting d10, Swimming d10, Throwing d8
Cha: –6; **Pace:** 7; **Parry:** 7; **Toughness:** 16 (6)
Hindrances: Bloodthirsty, Mean, Loyal
Edges: Combat Reflexes, Improved Frenzy, Strong Willed
Gear: Combat armor (+6, –4 AP), 2× fusion grenades (Range 5/10/20, Damage 3d8, AP 2), pulse rifle (Range 20/40/80, Damage 3d6, AP 4, RoF 1).
Special Abilities:
- **Attack, Melee:** Damage Str+2d6, AP 2. (Psionic bite / claw.)
- **Aquatic:** Pace 10.
- **Bite/Claws:** Str+d6.
- **Fearless:** Tharn are immune to fear and Intimidation.
- **Resistance (Psionics):** Tharn add +4 to rolls made to resist psionic effects and suffer only half damage from attacks.
- **Size +3:** Tharn stand nine feet tall and are nothing but muscle and teeth.

NEVERMORE

Batson Gray was once the Raven, sidekick to the Owl. After his mentor was slain, he took on the aspect of Nevermore and is willing to kill *if* he has no alternative. He allows his foes to think he kills much more indiscriminately.

Attributes: Agility d12+2, Smarts d10, Spirit d10, Strength d10, Vigor d10
Skills: Climbing d12, Driving d10, Fighting d12+2, Healing d10, Intimidation d10, Knowledge (Mechanical Engineering) d6, Notice d10, Persuasion d6, Piloting d10, Repair d8, Shooting d8, Stealth d12, Streetwise d10, Survival (Urban) d10, Swimming d10, Taunt d8 Throwing d10
Cha: +2; **Pace:** 6; **Parry:** 14; **Toughness:** 11 (4)
Hindrances: Code of Honor, Heroic, Loyal, Vengeful (Major)
Edges: Acrobat, Attractive, Block, Combat Reflexes, Combat Sense, Counterattack, Improved Dodge, Elan, Extraction, First Strike, Harder to Kill, Improvisational Fighter, Improved Sweep, Martial Artist
Gear: Body armor (+4, –4 AP), staff (Str+d6).
Special Abilities:
- **Heightened Senses:** Device. Infravision. Low Light Vision. (Goggles.)
- **Parry+3:** Device. Deflect. Protector. (Staff.)
- **Stun:** Contingent on successful Fighting attack. Device. (Staff.)
- **Super Attribute:** Agility +3.
- **Super Skill:** Fighting +2.
- **Swinging:** Device. Strong Line. (Grappling hook.)
- **Uncanny Reflexes:** –2 to hit. Blinding Reflexes. (Leaping and jumping.)

NIGHT COURT

The Night Court consists of three super powered beings supported by ordinary gangers called the Lynch Mob.

THE JUDGE

BOWERY

Corben Malone, formerly the heroic Battlin' Judge of Long Island, now prosecutes his particular brand of justice on any criminals who cross his path. He wears a black commando oufit and full face mask that symbolizes "blind justice."

Attributes: Agility d8, Smarts d10, Spirit d12, Strength d12+2, Vigor d12
Skills: Climbing d10, Driving d8, Fighting d12, Healing d6, Intimidation d10, Investigation d8, Knowledge (Battle) d10, Knowledge (Law) d10, Notice d8, Persuasion d6, Repair d6, Shooting d12, Stealth d10, Streetwise d6, Survival d6, Swimming d8, Throwing d8
Cha: –2; **Pace:** 6; **Parry:** 10; **Toughness:** 16 (4)
Hindrances: Mean, Ruthless (Major), Stubborn, Vengeful (Major), Vow (Major: Clean up New York City!)

Edges: Alertness, Improved Block, Brave, Brawny, Combat Reflexes, Improved Counterattack, Dead Shot, Improved Extraction, Improved First Strike, Harder to Kill, Killer Instinct, Improved Level Headed, Marksman, Nerves of Steel

Gear: Pulse Assault Rifle (Range 20/40/80, Damage 3d6, AP 4, RoF 3), underslung grenade launcher (frag grenades, Range 24/48/96, Damage 3d6, MBT, 6 shots), body armor (+4).

Super Powers:

- **Absorption:** Metal. The Judge absorbs bullets, blades, and other metal attacks on his rock hard skin.
- **Extra Actions:** The Judge has lightning fast reflexes.
- **Fear:** The Judge "judges" his foes and condemns them to death for their defiance.
- **Fearless:** Corben knows no fear.
- **Negation:** Full Spectrum. Contingent on a failed Fear test from his Fear power. The "judged" lose their powers temporarily. Ranged Touch attack.
- **Super Attribute:** Strength +3, Vigor +2.
- **Toughness +3:** The Judge has rock hard skin.
- **Uncanny Reflexes:** Attacks against the Judge suffer a −4 penalty as long as he isn't taken by surprise.

JURY

Shari Vanover was a court clerk in the same district where Corben worked. She quietly fell in love with the handsome major and followed his exploits when he fought the k'tharen. When he went missing, she went into a state of dread and despair. When Shari heard he was alive, she vowed to dark powers that she would do anything to protect him. She changed that night into Jury, a mind-shattering psychic with an undying love for Corben *and* his cause.

In combat, Shari turns and locks down the physically tough foes while Judge or Executioner dispatches the rest. Then they concentrate on the "big guys."

Attributes: Agility d8, Smarts d8, Spirit d10, Strength d8, Vigor d8

Skills: Driving d6, Fighting d6, Healing d6, Indimitation d6, Investigation d6, Knowledge (Law) d6, Notice d10, Persuasion d6, Shooting d8, Stealth d6

Cha: +2; **Pace:** 6; **Parry:** 5; **Toughness:** 6

Hindrances: Loyal, Ruthless (Major), Vow (Major. Protect the Judge with her life)

Edges: Attractive, Mentalist

Gear: None.

Super Powers:

- **Attack, Ranged:** Range 24/48/96, Damage 4d6, RoF 1. Area Effect (LBT). (Psychic blast.) When Jury uses the Area Effect option, she calls it the "Condemnation of 12," based on a typical jury of the court.
- **Awareness:** Jury can sense thoughts all around her, eliminating all Gang Up bonuses.
- **Chameleon:** Voice. Few know that Jury sometimes infiltrates the Judge's enemies to learn their plans.
- **Danger Sense:** Jury senses most thoughts directed at her or her companions.
- **Deflection 5:** Psychic shield. Requires Activation.
- **Flight:** Pace 12, Climb 0.
- **Mind Control:** In combat, Jury uses this power to turn the largest and least intellectual foe against his companions.
- **Mind Reading:** Jury knows what evil lurks in the hearts of the accused.
- **Paralysis:** Strong. Jury can lock down troublesome foes with a contest of Smarts.
- **Telekinesis 1:** Jury has minor telekinetic powers. Strength d10, Range 12".

EXECUTIONER

The Executioner appeared soon after Jury came to the Judge's side. It's possible he's a manifestation of the Judge's psyche—or more likely Jury's! Whatever the case, his material form can be defeated, though he seems to return the following night no matter how grievous the injury. Once he was even burned to cinders and returned the next day. Whether he's a ghost or a figment of Judge or Jury's imagination, he's the deadliest of the three.

Attributes: Agility d8, Smarts d8(A), Spirit d10, Strength d12, Vigor d10

Skills: Fighting d10, Notice d8

Cha: 0; **Pace:** 6; **Parry:** 7; **Toughness:** 7

Hindrances: Distinctive Apperance (the Executioner only appears in his costumed form), Loyal, Power Negation (the Executioner does not manifest if Judge and Jury aren't alive *and* conscious), Quirk (Never Speaks)

Edges: Improved Sweep

Gear: None.

Super Powers:

- **Altered Form:** Darkness. The Executioner is a being of dark justice. He appears physical and can be hurt normally, but suffers no additional damage from called shots or falling.
- **Attack, Melee:** Damage Str+4d6, AP 4, Focus, Heavy Weapon, Lethal, Reach. Major Limitation (The scythe does half damage to "heroes" or other "good" people. Game Master's call.) (Scythe of pure darkness.)
- **Awareness:** The Executioner ignores obscurement penalties and ignores Gang Up bonuses from the guilty. And *everyone* is guilty.
- **Damage Field:** Darkness. Damage 2d6. The guilty burn with dark fire in the presence of the Executioner. Major Limitation (No damage to "heroes" or other "good" people. Game Master's call.)
- **Doesn't Breathe:** The Executioner has passed sentence on the air itself, and needs it not.
- **Doesn't Eat:** The Executioner feeds on justice!
- **Fear:** Terror. The Executioner points his scythe at the guilty before moving to pass final sentence. Major Limitation (One foe only, has no effect on "good" characters. GM's call.)
- **Fearless:** The Exectioner knows no fear.
- **Flight:** Pace 6, Climb 0. The Executioner wafts slowly and inevitably toward the accused.
- **Intangibility:** Phase. The Executioner appears solid enough, but is actually made of pure darkness. He is vulnerable, however, to light, fire, or the attacks of good people and "heroes" (GM's call).
- **Regeneration 1:** Regrowth. The Executioner returns night after night as long as both Judge and Jury are alive and consciouss. If defeated, he vanishes into dark mist and returns when sun sets the next day.

THE RED HAND

Prior to the invasion the Red Hand was spread throughout the world and had a number of super-powered agents in their employ. When the New York crime families got wiped out during the invasion—or fled—one of the more vicious capos, Tony "Iron Head" Marinaro, stepped up.

IRON HEAD TONY

Tony likes to tell people he has a steel skull, but really that's just a ploy to keep people from shooting him there instead of the bulletproof vest he wears! In fact, his *mother* gave him the knickname when he was younger because he was so stubborn.

Attributes: Agility d8, Smarts d10, Spirit d10, Strength d8, Vigor d8

Skills: Driving d10, Fighting d8, Gambling d8, Intimidation d10, Knowledge (Business) d8, Notice d10, Repair d6, Shooting d8, Stealth d8, Streetwise d10, Swimming d6, Taunt d8, Throwing d4

Cha: 0; **Pace:** 6; **Parry:** 7; **Toughness:** 10 (4)

Hindrances: Mean, Greedy (Minor), Stubborn, Vengeful

Edges: Block, Charismatic, Combat Reflexes, Command, Dead Shot, Elan, Hard to Kill, Leader of Men, Improved Level Headed, Improved Nerves of Steel

Gear: Body armor (+4, −4 AP), pulse pistol (Range 10/20/40, Damage 2d6, AP 2, RoF 1).

ENFORCER

Tony's Enforcers are mostly thugs from before the war. Some were his captains and a few got promoted when the casualties started piling up. They're mostly stereotypical wise guys, but a few of the tougher females (including some widows) have joined the ranks as well. "I'm egalitarian," Tony likes to say of his capos.

Attributes: Agility d6, Smarts d8, Spirit d8, Strength d8, Vigor d8

Skills: Driving d8,

Fighting d8, Gambling d8, Intimidation d8, Investigation d6, Lockpicking d6, Notice d8, Persuasion d8, Stealth d8

Cha: −2; **Pace:** 6; **Parry:** 6; **Toughness:** 10 (4)

Hindrances: Greedy (Minor), Mean

Edges: The GM should choose a couple of specialities for each Enforcer.

Gear: Body armor (+4, −4 AP), pulse SMG (Range 10/20/40, Damage 2d6, AP 2, RoF 3).

THUG

Being a thug for the Red Hand is the most stable work a person can get in the NYCP. They get consistent food, water, and shelter, which is more than most anyone else can claim these days.

Attributes: Agility d6, Smarts d4, Spirit d6, Strength d6, Vigor d6

Skills: Climbing d4, Driving d6, Fighting d6, Gambling d4, Intimidation d6, Notice d6, Persuasion d4, Shooting d6, Stealth d6, Streetwise d6, Survival (Urban) d6, Swimming d4, Throwing d4

Cha: −2; **Pace:** 6; **Parry:** 5; **Toughness:** 5

Hindrances: Greedy (Minor), Mean

Edges: —

Gear: Most carry a piece of rebar (Str+d6), but they're occasionally armed with more potent weapons such as pistols, rifles, and shotguns as Tony sees fit.

SCAVENGERS

These are those unfortunate adult men and women who were left behind and don't have the bravado, aggression, or combat skills of the gangers.

Loot: Roll a d6 per member of the group if defeated, cowed, or robbed. The roll may Ace. The total is the amount of scavenged valuables they have on them in dollars. Most scav bands have twice that in their lair. Seven scavs, for example, have 7d6 × $1 in goods on their person, split between them.

SCAV

Scavs also tend to have trade or Knowledge skills relevant to their former life.

Attributes: Agility d6, Smarts d4, Spirit d6, Strength d6, Vigor d6

Skills: Fighting d4, Notice d6, Stealth d6

Pace: 6; **Parry:** 4; **Toughness:** 5

Hindrances: —

Edges: —

Gear: Most scavs carry small knives or clubs (Str+d4). Some might occasionally have a firearm of the GM's choice, but most sell weaponry to the Red Hand.

SHIVER

This former martial artist isn't at all what he appears to be. He's actually Nevermore! The clever martial artist and crime fighter wanders several neighborhoods in different guises so he can keep tabs on the city's most important players. Shiver is just one of his many aliases.

That said, working with Shiver an hour or so a day for three weeks total gives a character the Martial Artist Edge (one time only). If a character already has it, Shiver's training gives the character +1 Parry—against everyone *but* Nevermore since he knows the "student's" maneuvers!

SHRILL

Janet Willows discovered her mutant talents while training to be an opera singer. She was auditioning for a part when she tried to hit a high note she'd never hit before—and destroyed the auditorium!

Janet tried to apologize but the opera world would have nothing to do with "the freak." After some poisonous soul-searching, she decided that if she couldn't achieve fame and fortune legitimately, she'd do it as Shrill—a super villain.

Attributes: Agility d8, Smarts d8, Spirit d8, Strength d4, Vigor d8

Skills: Fighting d6, Knowledge (Opera) d6, Lockpicking d8, Notice d6, Shooting d8, Stealth d8

Cha: +2; **Pace:** 6; **Parry:** 5; **Toughness:** 6

Gear: None.

Hindrances: Delusional (Minor—people love a villain), Greedy (Minor)

Edges: Arcane Background (Super Powers), Charismatic

Special Abilities:

- **Deflection:** Requires Activation. −6 to hit with ranged attacks. (Wall of sound.)
- **Energy Control:** Sound.
- **Heightened Senses:** Infravision, Low Light Vision, Spatial Sense. (Sonar.)
- **Intangibility:** Phase. (Shrill can transform into an acoustic vibration.)
- **Stun:** Area Effect (MBT), Ranged Touch Attack 12" (Shooting). (Shrill scream.)

SYKOS

The Sykos number about 10,000 gangers and 1,000 scavengers. They are truly the worst dregs of the city, but those still present are at least hardy survivors.

A Syko band always has a gang leader for every dozen gangers or scavs. They only get a super-powered escort for special missions or when found in groups of 20.

BIG SIS

Carolyn Jones was a nurse working various trauma centers throughout Manhattan for the last decade. One day, while cleaning up one of the Guardian's messes in Times Square, she inhaled a strange mist left behind by one of the hero's many archenemies. Over the next few months, Carolyn began to change. She developed super strength, cunning, and a desire for mayhem and violence. Thus was born Big Sis!

Attributes: Agility d10, Smarts d10, Spirit d10, Strength d12+6, Vigor d12+4

Skills: Climbing d6, Driving d6, Fighting d12+2, Healing d10, Intimidation d10, Investigation d8, Knowledge (Medicine) d8, Notice d10, Persuasion d8, Repair d4, Shooting d6, Stealth d10, Streetwise d12, Swimming d6, Taunt d10, Throwing d10

Cha: +2; **Pace:** 6; **Parry:** 14; **Toughness:** 15

Hindrances: Cautious, Delusional (Major—The Grim Reaper is real and killing calls his attention), Mean, Ruthless (Minor)

Edges: Very Attractive

Gear: —

Special Abilities:

- **Attack, Melee:** Damage Str+6d6. Focus. Device. (Sledge hammer.)
- **Chameleon:** Voice. (Big Sis often uses this ability to gather intel and surprise her foes.)
- **Leaping:** Sis can jump up to 4" (8 yards) straight up and 8" (16 yards) flat-footed. She often uses this to jump onto rooftops and escape more powerful foes.
- **Parry +5:** Super reflexes.
- **Regeneration:** Big Sis rolls to regenerate once per day. Regrowth.
- **Super Attribute:** Strength +9. Vigor +8.
- **Super Skill:** Fighting +4.
- **Toughness +5:** Big Sis is built like a gymnast but is infused with strange energy that gives her super *toughness*.

TINY APHRODITE

A villain called the Puppeteer had a host of android servants. One of them was known in super villain circles as a powerful fighter—and perhaps an intimate companion of the strange puppet master. Buried in the ruins is the android body of this servant. If disturbed, she comes to life, damaged and ready to fight.

Tiny Aphrodite has two wounds that require a workshop, tools, and a Repair roll to fix. She's loyal to the Puppeteer and must be reprogrammed to serve another. This can only be done while she's Incapacitated, and requires a d4 days for each attempt at a Knowledge (Electronics) roll at −4.

Attributes: Agility d8, Smarts d6, Spirit d10, Strength d12+2, Vigor d10

Skills: Climbing d8, Fighting d10, Notice d4

Cha: +2; **Pace:** 6; **Parry:** 6; **Toughness:** 17 (6)

Hindrances: Mean

Edges: Very Attractive

Gear: —

Special Abilities:

- **Armor +6:** Tiny Aphrodite is made of very tough composite materials.
- **Attack, Melee:** Damage Str+2d6. Focus. Tiny Aphrodite packs a powerful punch!
- **Construct:** +2 to recover from being Shaken; doesn't breathe; immune to disease and poison; ignores one level of wound penalties.
- **Size −1:** Tiny Aphrodite is about 4' tall.
- **Super Attribute:** Strength +2.
- **Toughness +5:** The puppet is a durable piece of work.

THE VERMINTIDE

This strange creature is actually some sort of strange fungus that has infected 90% of the rat population in New York City. The thing originated on another world conquered by the v'sori, a cosmic hitchhiker that found a natural host in the massive rat population.

The Vermintide "lives" in millions of rats, but it has a central consciousness that lives in a larger, mutated, and far more feral strain at the center. It can see and hear through all its vestigial swarms, but this requires effort and attention—it is not automatic, and with thousands of swarms and millions of rats under its control it can take the Vermintide a while to notice even direct attacks against it. When it does notice an attack, it either sends in practically endless wave of reinforcements to overwhelm its prey, or retreats if its member swarms are perishing quickly.

Most times the Vermintide is encountered, it's composed of 2d6 swarms—a deadly tidal wave of chittering rats that can strip most foes to bone in minutes. If the swarms are defeated (or evaded) within 10 rounds, no further reinforcements are sent. If the fight lasts longer than that, the Vermintide sends another 1d6 swarms every five rounds until either half of all the swarms are dispersed or the foes are dead.

If the Vermintide itself is involved, add the more powerful core swarm listed below.

VERMINTIDE SWARM

Attributes: Agility d10, Smarts d6 (A), Spirit d12, Strength d8, Vigor d10
Skills: Notice d6
Pace: 8; **Parry:** 4; **Toughness:** 7
Special Abilities:

- **Bite:** The rats inflict hundreds of tiny bites every round, hitting automatically and causing 2d4 damage to everyone in the template. Damage is applied to the victim's least armored location.
- **Split:** Vermintide swarms start as Medium Burst Templates. When wounded, they split into two smaller swarms (Small Burst Template) of Toughness 5.
- **Swarm:** Parry +2 (already figured in, above). Cutting, piercing, and single shot weapons kill individual creatures but do no damage to the swarm as a whole. Area-effect attacks and blunt weapons cause damage normally (including raw Strength / stomp attacks).

VERMINTIDE CORE SWARM

The core of the swarm is clearly different than the rest of the rodents. The rats are jet black with glowing red eyes and jagged, white teeth.

The core acts as a normal swarm, but as a Wild Card has three wounds—including after it splits.

Attributes: Agility d10, Smarts d6 (A), Spirit d12, Strength d8, Vigor d10
Skills: Notice d6
Pace: 8; **Parry:** 4; **Toughness:** 7
Special Abilities:

- **Bite:** The rats inflict hundreds of tiny bites every round, hitting automatically and causing 2d4 damage to everyone in the template. Damage is applied to the victim's least armored location.
- **Split:** Vermintide swarms start as Medium Burst Templates. When wounded, they split into two smaller swarms (Small Burst Template) of Toughness 5.
- **Swarm:** Parry +2 (already figured in, above). Cutting, piercing, and single shot weapons kill individual creatures but do no damage to the swarm as a whole. Area-effect attacks and blunt weapons cause damage normally (including raw Strength/ stomp attacks).

V'SORI

Below are typical examples of the alien invaders who conquered the Earth. Of course individuals vary greatly, but this template should serve as a base.

Here's a quick reminder of the v'sori heirarchy.

- The **Overmind** is the supreme ruler of the v'sori.
- **War Master F'arak** is responsible for conquering Earth.
- Seven **Shock Lords** serve the War Master, two for Asia, none for Antarctica, and one each for the other continents.
- **Overlords** are administrators for nation-size regions.
- **Warlords** watch over districts. Warlord Sh'tarka is responsible for the New England area, including the New York City Prison.
- **Battle Masters** are elite v'sori shock troops.
- **Solos** are v'sori with a few very powerful abilities.
- **Soldiers** make up the v'sori home legions.
- **K'tharen** (fins) make up the bulk of the v'sori troops on Earth, along with hundreds of thousands of **drones** and **hyper-drones.**

BATTLE MASTER

Elite Battle Masters are powerful foes. They're used for special operations or to kill or capture super powered foes. They often follow behind k'tharen wave attacks, letting the fins absorb the bulk of the enemy's counterattack.

A typical squad is eight Battle Masters, one of which is a leader with the Command and Tactician Edges.

Attributes: Agility d8, Smarts d8, Spirit d6, Strength d8, Vigor d8

Skills: Fighting d10, Intimidation d8, Knowledge (Tactics) d6, Notice d8, Persuasion d8, Shooting d10, Stealth d8, Swimming d10, Taunt d8

Cha: –2; **Pace:** 6; **Parry:** 7; **Toughness:** 12 (6)

Hindrances: Mean, Ruthless (Major)

Edges: Combat Reflexes, Combat Sense, First Strike, Level Headed

Gear: Combat armor (+6, –4 AP), 2×fusion grenades (Range 5/10/20, Damage 3d8, AP 2), pulse rifle (Range 20/40/80, Damage 3d6, AP 4, RoF 1).

Special Abilities:

- **Aquatic:** Pace 10.
- **Attack, Ranged:** (Range 12/24/48, Damage 2d6, AP 4. Cone. (Mind Blast).
- **Low Light Vision:** V'sori ignore penalties for Dim and Dark lighting.
- **Stun:** Large Burst Template, Smarts roll or be Shaken. (Synaptic shock psionic blast).
- **Telepathy:** Limited. V'sori can communicate telepathically with other v'sori, Atlanteans, or Atlantean hybrids.

SCIENTIST

V'sori scientists are cruel, curious creatures. They are kept well away from battle, but have access to typical armor and weapons if desired.

Attributes: Agility d6, Smarts d12, Spirit d8, Strength d6, Vigor d6

Skills: Fighting d4, Intimidation d8, Knowledge (Biology) d12, Knowledge (Chemistry) d10, Knowledge (Engineering) d12, Notice d12, Persuasion d8, Repair d12, Shooting d6, Swimming d10, Taunt d10

Cha: 0; **Pace:** 6; **Parry:** 4 **Toughness:** 5

Hindrances: Curious, Ruthless (Major)

Edges: Mr. Fix It, Scholar

Gear: Datapad.

Special Abilities:

- **Aquatic:** Pace 10.
- **Attack, Ranged:** (Range 12/24/48, Damage 2d6, AP 4. Cone. (Mind Blast).
- **Low Light Vision:** V'sori ignore penalties for Dim and Dark lighting.
- **Stun:** Large Burst Template, Smarts roll or be Shaken. (Synaptic shock psionic blast).
- **Telepathy:** Limited. V'sori can communicate telepathically with other v'sori, Atlanteans, or Atlantean hybrids.

SHOCK LORD

Shock Lords are schemers with a mind for strategy and propaganda and a cruel streak a contintent wide. They also tend to be a little older, but have more than made up for their fading physical abilities with cunning and experience.

Shock Lords are kept well away from threats so they don't normally wear armor, but have access to whatever gear they want if threatened.

Attributes: Agility d6, Smarts d12, Spirit d10, Strength d6, Vigor d6

Skills: Fighting d8, Intimidation d10, Investigation d10, Knowledge (Politics) d10, Notice d8, Persuasion d6, Shooting d6, Swimming d10, Taunt d8

Cha: 0; **Pace:** 6; **Parry:** 6; **Toughness:** 5

Hindrances: Mean, Monologuer, Ruthless (Major)

Edges: Charismatic, Danger Sense, Investigator, Mentalist

Gear: Datapad.

Special Abilities:

- **Aquatic:** Pace 10.
- **Attack, Ranged:** (Range 12/24/48, Damage 3d6, AP 4. Cone. (Mind Blast).
- **Force Control 3:** d12+1. Area Effect. Force Field. Heavy Weapon. Range 24".
- **Low Light Vision:** V'sori ignore penalties for Dim and Dark lighting.
- **Mind Control:** Range 12". Multiple Minds.
- **Mind Reading:** Range 12".
- **Stun:** Large Burst Template, Smarts roll or be Shaken. (Synaptic shock psionic blast).
- **Telekinesis:** Strength d12, Range 12".
- **Telepathy:** Limited. V'sori can communicate telepathically with other v'sori, Atlanteans, or Atlantean hybrids.

SOLDIER

V'sori soldiers are well-trained and loyal to the Warlord. They don't get along with the elite Battle Masters.

Attributes: Agility d8, Smarts d8, Spirit d6, Strength d6, Vigor d6

Skills: Fighting d8, Intimidation d8, Notice d6, Shooting d8, Stealth d6, Swimming d10, Taunt d6

Cha: –2; **Pace:** 6; **Parry:** 6; **Toughness:** 11 (6)

Hindrances: Mean

Edges: Combat Sense

Gear: Combat armor (+6, –4 AP), 2× fusion grenades (Range 5/10/20, Damage 3d8, AP 2), pulse SMG (Range 10/20/40, Damage 2d6, AP 2, RoF 3).

Special Abilities:

- **Aquatic:** Pace 10.
- **Low Light Vision:** V'sori ignore penalties for Dim and Dark lighting.
- **Telepathy:** Limited. V'sori can communicate telepathically with other v'sori, Atlanteans, or Atlantean hybrids.

SOLO

Not all v'sori have a wide range of powers; those with a single strong psionic talent are called Solos. Many of these mentalists hone their single skill to its full potential, becoming ruthless and feared interrogators, detainment camp overseers, or other specialists.

Use the statistics for Battle Masters but add one or more of the following powers:

- **Attack, Ranged:** (Range 12/24/48, Damage 4d6, AP 4. Cone. (Mind Blast).
- **Force Control 2:** d12. Area Effect. Force Field.
- **Illusion 4:** 5" (10 yard) diameter sphere.
- **Mind Control:** Range 12". Multiple Minds.
- **Telekinesis:** Strength d12, Range 12".

WARLORD

Attributes: Agility d8, Smarts d8, Spirit d6, Strength d6, Vigor d8

Skills: Fighting d10, Intimidation d8, Knowledge (V'sori Politics) d8, Notice d8, Persuasion d8, Shooting d10, Swimming d10, Taunt d8

Cha: –2; **Pace:** 6; **Parry:** 7; **Toughness:** 12 (6)

Hindrances: Mean, Ruthless (Minor)

Edges: Combat Reflexes, Command, Inspire, Natural Leader

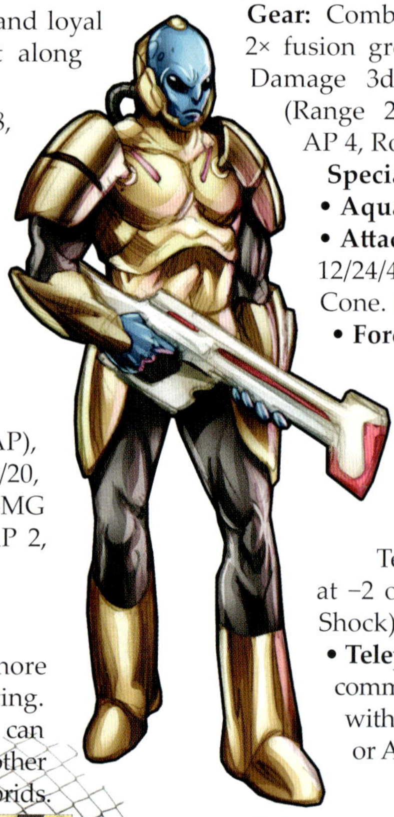

Gear: Combat armor (+6, –4 AP), 2× fusion grenades (Range 5/10/20, Damage 3d8, AP 2), pulse rifle (Range 20/40/80, Damage 3d6, AP 4, RoF 1).

Special Abilities:

- **Aquatic:** Pace 10.
- **Attack, Ranged:** (Range 12/24/48, Damage 2d6, AP 4. Cone. (Mind Blast).
- **Force Control 2:** d12. Area Effect. Force Field.
- **Low-Light Vision:** V'sori ignore penalties for Dim and Dark lighting.
- **Stun:** Large Burst Template, Smarts roll at –2 or be Shaken. (Synaptic Shock).
- **Telepathy:** Limited. V'sori can communicate telepathically with other v'sori, Atlanteans, or Atlantean hybrids.

WAR MASTER

F'arak is the War Master of Earth, and the most powerful and cunning v'sori in our solar system.

Attributes: Agility d10, Smarts d10, Spirit d8, Strength d8, Vigor d10

Skills: Fighting d12, Intimidation d8, Investigation d8, Knowledge (V'sori Politics) d12, Notice d10, Persuasion d6, Shooting d8, Swimming d10

Cha: –2; **Pace:** 6; **Parry:** 8; **Toughness:** 13 (6)

Hindrances: Mean, Ruthless (Major)

Edges: Combat Reflexes, Command, Inspire, Natural Leader

Gear: Combat armor (+6, –4 AP), 2×fusion grenades (Range 5/10/20, Damage 3d8, AP 2), pulse rifle (Range 20/40/80, Damage 3d6, AP 4, RoF 1).

Special Abilities:

- **Aquatic:** Pace 10.
- **Attack, Ranged:** (Range 12/24/48, Damage 2d6, AP 4. Cone. (Mind Blast).
- **Force Control 3:** d12+1. Area Effect. Force Field. Heavy Weapon. Range 24".
- **Low Light Vision:** V'sori ignore penalties for Dim and Dark lighting.
- **Mind Control:** Range 12". Multiple Minds.
- **Mind Reading:** Range 12".
- **Stun:** Large Burst Template, Smarts roll or be Shaken. (Synaptic shock psionic blast).
- **Telekinesis:** Strength d12, Range 12".
- **Telepathy:** Limited. V'sori can communicate telepathically with other v'sori, Atlanteans, or Atlantean hybrids.

DRONES

Drones are encased in form-fitting body armor with visored helmets. They bristle with weaponry and cables carrying fluids and wiring to their various systems.

See the free online supplement *Necessary Evil: The Alien Update*, for statistics on Hyper Drones.

DRONE

Attributes: Agility d6, Smarts d4, Spirit d6, Strength d10, Vigor d8

Skills: Driving d6, Fighting d8, Intimidation d6, Notice d4, Shooting d8, Swimming d6

Pace: 6; **Parry:** 6; **Toughness:** 8 (2)

Hindrances: —

Edges: Combat Reflexes

Gear: —

Special Abilities:

- **Ambidextrous:** Drones have no off-hand penalty.
- **Aquatic:** Pace 6. Cybernetic gills and marine adaptations allow drones to function underwater.
- **Armor +2:** Cybernetic implant armor.
- **Attack, Melee:** Damage Str+d6, AP 2. Heavy Weapon. (Vibro claws.)
- **Attack, Ranged:** Range 12/24/48, Damage 3d6, AP 4, RoF 1.
- **Fearless:** Drones are immune to Fear and Intimidation.
- **Heightened Senses:** Low Light Vision. (Cybernetic eyes.)
- **Stun:** Strong. (Electro shock.)

WAR SPHERES

When there isn't enough of a rebel's body left to turn it into a standard drone, v'sori scientists make the best of what's left. War spheres are floating, metallic drones the size of beach balls with short retractable arms for simple tasks.

Located in the center of a war sphere's well-armored shell is the still-living brain of the rebel subject, wiped and cybernetically controlled in exactly the same way as standard drones.

Attributes: Agility d10, Smarts d4, Spirit d6, Strength d10, Vigor d6

Skills: Driving d6, Fighting d6, Intimidation d6, Notice d8, Shooting d8

Pace: —; **Parry:** 5; **Toughness:** 10 (6)

Special Abilities:

- **Armor +6:** Heavy Armor. War spheres are encased in thick metal.
- **Attack, Ranged:** Range 12/24/48, Damage 4d6, AP 4, RoF 1. (Blasters.)
- **Construct:** +2 to recover from being Shaken; doesn't breathe; immune to disease and poison; ignores one level of wound penalties.
- **Fearless:** Drones are immune to Fear and Intimidation.
- **Flight:** Pace 12.
- **Heightened Senses:** Infravision. Low Light Vision. (Cybernetic eyes.)
- **Size –1:** War spheres are about the size of a large beach ball.